Looking Good, Eating Right

Looking Good, Eating Right

A SENSIBLE GUIDE
TO PROPER NUTRITION AND
WEIGHT LOSS FOR TEENS

BY DR. CHARLES A. SALTER

THE MILLBROOK PRESS
BROOKFIELD, CONNECTICUT
A TEEN NUTRITION BOOK

I wish to acknowledge the support and assistance of my literary agent, Ms. Ruth Wreschner, and of my editor at The Millbrook Press, Ms. Maury Solomon. I also wish to thank Ms. Giuseppina Romano-Clarke for her assistance in collecting interview data.

Diagram by Anne Canevari Green

Cataloging-in-Publication Data

Salter, Charles A.

Looking good, eating right: a sensible guide to proper nutrition and weight loss for teens / by Charles A. Salter
p.; cm.—(Food and nutrition for young people)
Bibliography:
Includes index.

Summary: Useful information on eating disorders and eating habits for teenagers. Discusses the health hazards of being fat, the right and wrong ways to lose weight, and the value of exercise.
1. Weight control.   2. Eating disorders.   3. Diet
4. Exercise for weight control.   I. Title.   II. Series
ISBN 1-56294-047-3   1991   616.85 SAL

This book is affectionately dedicated to Jelia C. Witschi, R.D., my longtime nutrition teacher, mentor, colleague, and friend at Harvard University.

Contents

1

Help, I'm Getting Fat

Melissa was 13 and a freshman in high school when she first realized she had a problem. She had been gaining weight rapidly and was now 180 pounds. The mirror could no longer lie to her. Says Melissa, "I remember hating going to parties. I knew that I would spend most of the night in a corner because nobody would invite me to dance. I also knew that I couldn't eat anything because everybody would be watching me, to see if I was fat because I ate too much. I felt that I was better off at home reading a book. I hated myself, and I felt that everybody else was disgusted with me."

Melissa realized she was in trouble but didn't know what to do. She felt she couldn't turn to her parents. She felt it was their neglect and occasional teasing that made her this way to begin with. So she continued to suffer throughout her early teens. "My adolescence was terrible. I kept living in my shell, avoiding people my own age because I knew that they didn't like me. I was a very shy person, and my obesity did not help me at all. I used to go to gym classes already dressed in shorts, and I avoided taking showers afterward because I didn't want the other kids to see me naked."

Finally, after years of agony, Melissa found solace and help from people outside her family. "I was lucky to join a group of young people in my parish who accepted me for what I was. After being in the group for a few months, I fell in love with one of the boys. Amazingly, he liked me, too! All of a sudden I felt I was normal, and I decided that I wanted to do something about my weight. I went to a center where they measured my metabolism rate, checked my thyroid, and gave me a diet. The diet was easy to follow. I had a list of a large number of foods I could eat. I also started playing tennis and walking to school. I dropped my weight slowly but steadily."

Melissa did not have an easy time of it, however. She suffered several setbacks. "Later on, my boyfriend broke up with me, and I felt terrible. I was so depressed I started eating compulsively. It was then that I realized that my overweight and my eating behavior had something to do with my need to feel accepted and loved."

Armed with new insight, Melissa plunged right back into her diet and exercise program. Over a three-year period she lost 60 pounds, trimming down to 120. No one who sees her now would ever dream she was once fat. And the desperate loneliness is gone.

Do you ever feel like Melissa? Do you ever look in the mirror and worry about what you see? When you tuck in your chin, does that little flap of skin look like fat? Does the bulge you grab when you pinch your arm seem too thick?

If you don't think you're perfect, relax. No one else thinks he or she is perfect either. Even people you admire as terrific physical specimens, perhaps certain actors or models, probably in their own minds think they are too tall, too short, or too fat. One study found that about 80 percent even of 10- and 11-year-old girls had already tried dieting to lose what they thought was excess weight.

If you do feel a little overweight or downright fat, is there any hope?

Myths About Fat

Myth 1: If you think you're fat, you are. Not true. Most teens are too hard on themselves. In fact, one recent survey revealed that about 90 percent of teens thought they were too fat, though only about one quarter of these really were.

Myth 2: If you're born fat, you stay fat . . . period. Not so. Of all kids who are obese, only 14 percent become obese adults. That means that 86 percent don't! One way or the other, they are able to grow out of or conquer their problem.

Myth 3: If your parents have given you "fat genes," you're doomed. Though genetic factors do influence body type and size, inheritance is not destiny. The majority (59 percent) of kids with one obese and one normal-weight parent do not grow up to be obese themselves. Even a sizeable minority of kids with two obese parents do not become obese as they grow up. It may not be easy for them to become or remain slim, but 27 percent make it.

Myth 4: Diets for kids don't work. Some young people grow out of their overweight condition with no special effort. They hit their growth spurt, and their fat appears to just melt away as all their energy goes into building larger bones and muscles. Other young people must work to lose fat, however, and dieting can really help them. In one study, for instance, a group of overweight preteens attended a program in which they were taught better eating habits. By the end of 10 weeks, they lost an average of 6.5 percent of their excess weight. Within 2.5 years they averaged a loss of 29.1 percent. In another study, a group of obese teens went on a well-balanced diet and lost an average of 20.5 percent of their excess pounds in 16 months. If you have a weight problem, you can conquer it, too!

Myth 5: If you're skinny now, you've got it made. Many wish that were true. But as the teenage years come to an end, your metabolic rate (the rate at which you burn calories) slows down. In your preteen and early teen years, your metabolism may roar like a blast furnace, devouring every calorie of junk food you swallow. But over the years that furnace cools, allowing more and more of the excess energy you eat to turn to body fat. Even if you are skinny at 12 or 14, therefore, you can become overweight by 18 or 22 if you don't develop a healthy diet.

Myth 6: As long as you stay thin, it doesn't matter what you eat. False. Many teens stay thin by developing an eating disorder such as anorexia or bulimia. These disorders can be dangerous, even deadly. Other teens practice fad diets or eat too much junk food but stay thin due to a high metabolism rate. However, a poor diet may still make them feel weak or ill. It may affect their appearance and attractiveness, making them look worn out, sluggish, or apathetic. The wise teen wants to both look and feel good—and only a balanced diet can help with that.

RESOURCE CENTER
MEMORIAL PARKWAY JR. HIGH
KATY, TEXAS

No one's perfect, but some teens do have a definite weight problem that mars their appearance and may in time impair their health. How can you distinguish between a little harmless pudginess and the more serious problem of being obese?

Defining Beauty

There is no absolute standard of what is "normal" for human weight. Different cultures define normal weight in different ways. For instance, some native tribes (such as the Banyankole of East Africa) even today prize plumper women, while other cultures, such as our own, prefer thinner ones.

In fact, the same culture may vary over time. In the United States about a century ago, plumpness was considered a sign of beauty and health. But in the last couple of decades, our cultural definitions of normal thinness have steadily grown more extreme, particularly for women. Young women who win beauty pageants these days are typically thinner and lighter than those of only a few years ago. The same holds true for models. By today's standards, many of the "sex goddesses" in movies of the previous generation—for example, Marilyn

Monroe—would seem too fat now. Our culture today seems to demand that everyone fit the ideal of reedlike thinness. Famous people are often advised by "image consultants" to become as thin as possible. Rock stars such as Madonna and Laura Brannigan, for example, were much plumper in their earlier music videos. In more recent videos, they display the rigorous thinness that they believe their fans want. It may not seem fair, but our culture tolerates pudginess more on boys than on girls.

What is "normal," then, varies with time and place. However, there are now several ways to assess weight more objectively.

Defining Obesity

When actual body weight exceeds Ideal Body Weight (IBW) by 20 percent or more, physical health begins to suffer. So it makes sense to consider obesity as starting at this point.

Life insurance companies have calculated IBW by determining which adult body weights are associated with longer lifespans. For preteens and teenagers who are still growing, a related concept is the Reference Weight, or average weight for young people. Your Reference Weight is determined by taking into account your

TABLE 1
HEIGHT AND WEIGHT BY AGE
FOR TEENAGERS

Girls

Age	Average Height (in inches)	(Height Range*)	Average Weight (in pounds)	(Weight Range*)
12	60	(58–61.5)	92	(81–106)
12.5	61	(59–62.5)	97	(85–112)
13	62	(60.5–63.5)	102	(90–117)
13.5	62.5	(61–64.5)	107	(94–122)
14	63.5	(61.5–65)	111	(98–126)
14.5	63.5	(62–65.5)	115	(102–130)
15	64	(62–65.5)	118	(106–133)
15.5	64	(62–66)	121	(108–136)
16	64	(62.5–66)	123	(111–137)
16.5	64	(62.5–66)	125	(112–138)
17	64.5	(62.5–66)	125	(113–139)
17.5	64.5	(63–66)	125	(113–139)
18	64.5	(63–66)	125	(113–139)

Boys

Age	Average Height (in inches)	(Height Range*)	Average Weight (in pounds)	(Weight Range*)
12	59	(57–61)	88	(77–101)
12.5	60.5	(58–62.5)	93	(82–107)
13	61.5	(59.5–64)	99	(88–114)
13.5	63	(60.5–65)	106	(94–121)
14	64.5	(62–66.5)	112	(100–130)
14.5	65.5	(63–67.5)	119	(106–136)
15	66.5	(64.5–68.5)	125	(112–143)
15.5	67.5	(65.5–69.5)	131	(118–149)
16	68.5	(66.5–70)	137	(124–155)

TABLE 1 (Continued)

Age	Average Height (in inches)	(Height Range*)	Average Weight (in pounds)	(Weight Range*)
16.5	69	(67.5–71)	142	(129–160)
17	69.5	(68–71)	146	(133–164)
17.5	69.5	(68–71.5)	150	(136–166)
18	69.5	(68–71.5)	152	(138–168)

*This range covers the 25% of the population that fall just below the average and the 25% that fall just above it.

(Adapted from more extensive tables prepared by the National Center for Health Statistics, Health Resources Administration, U.S. Department of Health and Human Welfare.)

gender (male or female), age, and height. Reference Weights for teens are shown in Table 1.

How do you find your Reference Weight in Table 1? (We'll use the example of a girl who is 14 years old, is 65 inches tall, and weighs 128 pounds.) What is her Reference Weight (the standard to which she should compare herself)?

First, you should find the correct portion of the table for your gender (in this case, the girl's). Next, locate your current age (rounding off to the nearest half year) in the first column. Place a ruler or other straightedge across the row that corresponds to that age (in this case, age 14).

Look next at the average height for that age (63.5 inches in this case; remember that one foot equals 12 inches, so 63.5 inches equals 5 feet, 3.5 inches tall). If you are that height with your shoes off, stick to that line (our example is not). Note the average weight for that age and height. This is your Reference Weight.

If you are not of average height, don't worry. These are only average numbers and do not mean that you are abnormal if you don't fit them. There are two other ways to locate your height in the table. Just move the ruler up and down till you find that average height at another row. (In this case, you can't find 65 inches under the average height.) If you do find that height, note the average weight at that height regardless of your age. This is your Reference Weight.

If you can't find your height under the average height column, return to the row for your age. Look at the height-range column. If your height can be found in that range, stick with that row and look at the weight range (not the average weight). If your height still cannot be found, don't worry. About a quarter of teenagers are shorter than that range and a quarter are taller. Just move up and down the table, regardless of age, until you find the height range that includes you. (In this case, the 14-year-old girl can find her height of 65 inches in the range for age 14.) From the weight range, calculate your Reference Weight according to your height. (In this example, 65 is at the top of the height range for age 14, so take the top of the weight range, or 126, for the Reference Weight.) It gets a bit more difficult for heights in the middle of the range, but you can estimate by moving up one third on the weight range for every inch you move up on the height range. Ask an older friend, teacher, or parent to help you if you have trouble with this table.

Once you have your Reference Weight, compare your actual weight to it. (In this case, 128 is 2 pounds over the Reference Weight of 126.) If your weight is only a little over or under the Reference Weight, please relax! If it is 20 percent or more over your Reference Weight, you are considered overweight and should consult your family doctor.

When comparing yourself to any chart such as the Reference Weight one or an IBW chart for adults, you should keep in mind that these are average figures, not an absolute goal you must meet. "Ideal" in the case of the IBW chart refers to your chances, statistically speaking, of being in better health if you weigh in that range. It may or may not represent what you consider ideal in terms of your physical appearance in the mirror. If there is a large difference between what you consider your ideal weight to be and your Reference Weight, your concept of your ideal self may be distorted to an unhealthy extreme by adherence to our cultural definitions of ideal thinness.

As an example of how to calculate obesity, if your Reference Weight is 100 pounds, then more than 120 pounds is obese. The obesity point is merely the Reference Weight plus one fifth more.

There are some problems with this definition of obesity, however. For example, what about athletes such as Hulk Hogan and Joe Montana, not to mention weight-lifters such as Arnold Schwarzenegger? Athletic teens with plenty of solid muscle may weigh quite a bit more than their IBW, yet not be too fat by any stretch of the imagination.

For some other ways to estimate obesity, see Table 2.

Teenage Obesity

Unfortunately, obesity among teenagers appears to be on the rise. You might expect the opposite, with all the emphasis these days on appearance, on looking slender, on eating right, and on staying healthy. But, sad to say, national surveys of American children and teens indicate that the problem is growing steadily worse rather

TABLE 2
WAYS TO MEASURE OBESITY

Method for Measuring	What Is Obese?
Ideal Body Weight (IBW)	20% or more above IBW
Reference Weight	20% or more above the Reference Weight
Fat-fold test using calipers to measure (done by a professional)	More than 30% fat (girls) More than 25% fat (boys)
Pinch test (measure a pinch of belly skin with a ruler)	More than an inch
Waist-chest size (use a tape measure)	If waist circumference exceeds that of chest (male and female)
Floating test (float on back in a pool, then exhale)	If you don't sink, you're more than 25% fat

than better. The number of obese teens increased by 54 percent between 1963 and 1980. Today, about a quarter of teens are overweight.

Scientists have proposed several reasons for this sad increase in overweight teens. First, compared with past generations, the average teen today burns up fewer calories in work and exercise. Many spend their free time sitting around watching TV or playing computer games instead of engaging in physical activities such as riding bikes or playing sports.

And not only do teens typically exercise less these days, they also tend to spend more time on truly passive activities that further slow the rate at which they burn calories. One study[1] conducted at Harvard University, for example, found that the more hours of television watched per day, the more likely the viewer was to pack on excess weight. Excess TV robs young people of time for sports and exercise, and it burns even fewer calories than does homework or talking with friends. Plus, all those commercials for food tend to make viewers snack more, particularly on high-calorie treats. The shows themselves often portray favorite TV characters gorging on rich treats. For instance, Bill Cosby has often been shown munching on sugary doughnuts or high-calorie sandwiches even though his TV wife urges him to cut down on fat. The fictional alien ALF is constantly emptying the family larder as he pigs out on every kind of food.

The type of food chosen for snacks is another main reason for increasing obesity. Teens who grab a fresh carrot or apple for a snack are less likely to become overweight. But if the munchies send you hunting for chocolate fudge sundaes, caramel candy, cheesecake, chocolate chip cookies, and bags and bags of potato chips, sooner or later your body will start to expand. Most of these high-calorie treats have little nutritional value. Yet their consumption keeps increasing because people like the taste, whether the food is healthy for them or not. Also, in our rushed, time-pressured society, it's a lot easier to just chomp down a bag of chocolate and marshmallow cookies or cheese puffs than to fix a meal.

How This Book Can Help

You can reduce your level of body fat and keep it down. This book will show you the essentials of healthy dieting, steer you around the pitfalls of dangerous eating fads and disorders, and help you see where your life-style can be changed for maximum health benefit. To eat healthy and slim down does NOT mean that you have to starve or even deny yourself treats in every situation. Some fad diets and eating practices do call for self-starvation in one form or another, but that is not healthy. Other, generally safe diet plans may not be right for teens, who have different nutritional needs than adults.

The healthy way to achieve and maintain a normal body weight works best precisely because you do feed your body what it needs. Cravings and false feelings of hunger should diminish as you slowly adapt your body to a healthy eating plan.

Converting from a poor diet to a better one is not usually easy. It will take time and determination. You may suffer temporary setbacks. But the effort will certainly be worth it. A healthy diet helps you look better, feel better, and perform better. It makes you more attractive and boosts your self-confidence, both of which make you more desirable to others.

2

The Health Hazards of Obesity

Obesity can certainly harm physical health, but young people often feel the emotional and psychological burdens of overweight or obesity more acutely than the physical ones. Whereas serious physical damage due to obesity may take years to develop, the emotional price must often be paid immediately.

Living in a society that prizes physical thinness and shuns body fat can bring great pain to the overweight person. One study, for example, asked young people which of the following they would prefer as friends—a normal youth, one with a leg brace and crutches, one in a wheel chair, one with an amputated hand, one with facial disfigurement, and one who is obese. The obese youth was ranked lowest as a choice for a friend. Another study found that obese teens had as little as one-third the opportunity of their thinner classmates to get into college. A study of employers found that 16 percent refused to hire obese youth, and 44 percent more considered obesity a factor in not hiring them. As a result of all these social factors, many obese teens suffer a poor self-image. They experience feelings of shame, frustration, and inferiority. Some have serious problems adjusting to school or social situations.

Fair or not, we cannot realistically expect public opinion to change overnight. (An organization called the National Association to Aid Fat Americans, Inc.—NAAFA for short—has been working to change public attitudes since 1969, but not very successfully. Most teens have never even heard of it.) Until society does develop more tolerance of people who don't quite fit its definition of the ideal, however, the wise person will consider losing excess weight—or at least avoiding further weight gain—for the sake of his or her emotional as well as physical health.

Obese teens also have a greater chance of developing certain diseases. Every extra pound of fat just makes the problem worse.

But what are these diseases?

Heart
Disease

The circulatory system is composed of the heart, which pumps blood, and the complex network of vessels through which the blood runs. Arteries are the vessels that carry blood away from the heart, to enrich the body's organs with oxygen, nutrients, and water. They get smaller and smaller as they branch out among the various bodily tissues. Veins are the vessels that carry blood back toward the heart. Veins furthest from the heart are small, but as they approach the heart and join with other small veins, they grow larger and larger. Capillaries are the tiny vessels that connect the smallest arteries to the smallest veins, spreading blood throughout the tissues in the process. Since every living cell must have a continuous supply of fresh blood, anything that interrupts the blood flow can threaten health.

For instance, extra cholesterol—a form of fat—in the blood tends to get deposited within the lining of the arteries. These fatty deposits are called *plaques,* and when they clog the arteries the condition is called *atherosclerosis* (see illustration on page 30).

Artery openings are fairly narrow to begin with. An average artery is only about as wide as the tip of a pencil eraser or a cigarette. As the opening gets more and more clogged with fatty gunk, it gets harder and harder for the heart to pump blood through. This raises one's blood pressure. Worse, a small opening may suddenly become blocked (typically by a blood clot). If this happens in the artery that feeds the heart muscle, a heart "attack" results. If it happens in an

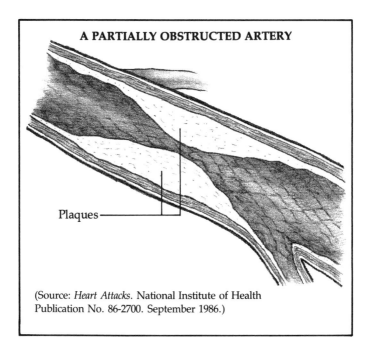

A PARTIALLY OBSTRUCTED ARTERY

Plaques

(Source: *Heart Attacks.* National Institute of Health Publication No. 86-2700. September 1986.)

artery feeding the brain, a stroke occurs. In either case, if the blockage is serious enough, the tissue normally fed by that artery can die, often impairing or even killing the person as a result.

What causes all this? A diet high in fat, which is also more likely to cause obesity, is one culprit. Your own liver converts much of the saturated fat that you've eaten into cholesterol. Saturated fat is most concentrated in meat and in coconut, palm, and palm kernel oils (the so-called "tropical" oils). A diet high in such fats increases your cholesterol level and the chances of developing serious atherosclerosis. Obesity itself contributes to heart disease. For instance, an obese person strains his or her heart by forcing it to pump blood through the extra miles of vessels grown in the excess fat tissue. All told, the more obese a person becomes, the worse the effects on the heart. As a rule of thumb, a 10 percent increase in weight increases the risk of getting heart disease by 30 percent.

Cancer Risk

Cancer is a dread and often fatal disease that can strike almost any organ in the body. In a typical case of cancer, the affected cells begin to multiply in an abnormal way. Rather than make more of the useful cells that normally go into that tissue, the cancerous cells begin producing useless cells that don't contribute anything to the body's activity. The cancerous mass of cells keeps expanding until it is removed through surgery or reduced in some way (by radiation or chemotherapy, for example), or until it causes serious and sometimes fatal damage.

How does this relate to obesity? The causes of cancer are usually not clear, though genetics, certain viruses, and environmental contaminants all seem to play a role. Another factor, one that clearly increases the risk of getting cancer, is obesity. Medical studies have revealed, for example, that obesity in men is linked to an increased risk of contracting cancer of the prostate (part of the male reproductive system) or of the colon and rectum. Obesity in women has been linked to an increased risk of cancer of the breast, ovaries, and uterus (all organs related to the female reproductive system) and also of the gallbladder. This is not to say that all overweight people will contract cancer, but obesity does increase the odds of doing so. Health experts are still debating just exactly how obesity increases cancer risk, but the fact that it does so is well documented.

Diabetes

Diabetes is a serious problem in which the body either can't produce enough of the hormone insulin or doesn't respond properly to the insulin that it does produce. If the problem persists too long undetected and unchecked, serious damage to a number of organs can result. For example, diabetes can contribute to circulatory system diseases, to blindness, and to nerve damage, particularly in the limbs.

The more severe form of diabetes, in which the pancreas can't produce enough insulin, occurs almost exclusively among preteens and teens younger than 15. It occurs equally among boys and girls, but it accounts for only 5 to 8 percent of all diabetes cases. Genetics plays a large role in this *juvenile-onset diabetes.*

The second major form of diabetes—*non-insulin-dependent diabetes*—almost always strikes overweight adults. Obese people are more likely to get it, to get it at a younger age, and to have it to a more serious degree. Why? Because increased body fat reduces the ability of the cells to respond to insulin, even though the pancreas may produce plenty of it. Although teens don't develop this form of diabetes at their age, they should realize that lack of control over their weight could greatly increase their risk of eventually getting it.

The obese diabetic (with the adult form of the disease) who loses even a little weight, however, can significantly lessen the severity of his or her diabetes. Many adults with this milder form of the problem can completely control it by returning to a normal body weight. (Children and teens with the severe form of the disease are not helped by weight loss, unfortunately.)

Other Diseases Linked With Obesity

Obesity helps cause or worsen many other diseases as well. Some of these may not be as life-threatening as the preceding ones, but they are still painful and can diminish one's life-style.

For instance, lugging around a lot of extra body weight tends to strain and eventually damage all the joints, particularly the knees and hips. It can worsen arthritis, even the juvenile kind that young people can get. It can increase the chances of falls and other accidents. When a joint or other bone injury does occur, being overweight makes healing slower and more difficult.

The gallbladder is the organ that stores bile, a liver secretion formed from cholesterol. Bile is important in the digestion of fat. Since obese people are generally processing more dietary fat, they tend to overuse this organ. Years of excess cholesterol formation, for instance, can lead to gallbladder problems such as gallstones, which often require surgery to eliminate.

Obesity and Disease Risk

Public health officials keep records of the major causes of the approximately 2 million deaths each year in the United States. Poor diet and obesity are linked to many of these major killer diseases. Note Table 3 on page 35. In this table the causes of death are arranged with those causing the most deaths listed first. In other words, cardiovascular diseases account for nearly half

TABLE 3
LEADING CAUSES OF DEATH
1987–88

Cause	Percentage of All Deaths
Cardiovascular diseases	44.8%
Cancer	22.5%
Lung diseases (pneumonia, emphysema)	7.3%
Accidents	4.5%
Diabetes	1.8%
Suicide	1.4%
All other causes combined	17.7%
Total:	100.0%

(Source: National Center for Health Statistics, U.S. Department of Health and Human Services.)

(44.8%) of all American deaths.* Cancer accounts for nearly a quarter (22.5%) of all deaths. Diabetes accounts for 1.8% of all deaths. These three major problems, which are all strongly linked to obesity and overall nutrition, together account for nearly three fourths (69.1%) of all deaths. The other three major causes of death may also be linked, at least partially, with obesity.

*These are figures for the entire population, regardless of age. During the teen years, death is more commonly caused by accidents, suicide, and homicide. But the obese teen who becomes an obese adult increases his or her chances of getting these diseases.

Excess fat can cut years off your life. Doctors estimate that for every inch that your waist size exceeds your chest size (measuring just below the bust in females), average life expectancy is cut by two years. In other words, males with a waist size about 5 inches greater than their chest size die about ten years earlier on the average than do trimmer men.

It may not be easy to lose your excess weight, but if you can, the effort will certainly pay off for you. Many studies show that those who lose excess weight can cut their excess risk of all these terrible diseases back to normal.

3

What Makes
   a Person Fat

Where does fat come from, anyway? The answer to that question can pave the way for understanding how we can best trim our bodies of excess fat.

Fat as
   Stored Energy

Every time you breathe, move, think, or exercise, you burn energy. Even when you are resting or asleep, the cells in your body continue to require energy to function. Without adequate supplies of energy, you would soon die.

Because of this ultimate biological fact, the body has two major mechanisms for storing energy for future use. For short-term storage of energy the body depends on *glycogen*, which consists of chains of glucose molecules (blood sugar). The body can store only a fairly small supply of glycogen—so little, in fact, that a marathon runner can burn up virtually his or her entire supply in a couple of hours.

Long-term reserve energy is stored primarily as body fat. The most common forms of body fat are called *triglycerides*. Each is composed of three smaller molecules of fatty acid (hence the prefix *"tri-"*) linked to a molecule of glycerol (hence the root word *"glyceride"*). These fat molecules come primarily from the fat in the food you eat. Your liver can also manufacture fat from the protein and carbohydrate you eat, but those processes require much more energy. Your body is most adept at storing body fat from dietary fat.

The body's potential for storing energy as body fat is virtually unlimited. In the absence of strenuous exercise, and without ingesting any further calories, the average person runs out of glycogen in a couple of days but can live off his or her fat store for one or two months. The *Guiness Book of World Records* lists the record for such a fast as being held by Angus Barbieri, who went 382 consecutive days without eating food, slimming down from 472 pounds to 178 pounds in the process. Thus, he lost 294 pounds at an average rate of about ¾ of a pound per day! (In long-term fasting or starvation, the body burns up much of its own muscle for fuel, too, which is why such fasts are extremely dangerous and require constant medical supervision.)

In humankind's distant past, and in poor countries now, this ability of the body to store reserve energy in the form of fat was, and still can be, life-saving. It can tide someone over in a period of famine until new sources of food become available. However, in modern societies where food is plentiful, this mechanism of energy storage causes more harm than good. Too much excess fat can rob years from your life, as we saw in the last chapter.

Sources of Energy

Excess calories available for conversion into body fat come from the energy-containing foods and beverages you consume. To compute how much energy that different foodstuffs can provide, see Table 4.

To understand this table, however, you must first know that a *calorie* is a basic unit of energy measurement. One calorie provides enough energy to raise the temperature of one kilogram (about a quart) of water one degree Celsius. (Technically, this is called a "kilocalorie," but most experts use the word "calorie" for short.)

TABLE 4
CALORIES IN VARIOUS NUTRIENTS

	Calories per	
Nutrient	Gram	Ounce
Fat (as in meat fat and vegetable oils)	9	255
Alcohol (as in whiskey, wine, beer)	7	199
Carbohydrate (as in sugars, grains, fruits, veggies)	4	114
Protein (as in lean meat, poultry, fish)	4	114

For instance, one medium apple provides about 100 calories, while a large cheeseburger with all the trimmings provides about 500 calories.

The Calorie-Fat Equivalence

There is one final piece to this puzzle—how the number of calories in the food you eat corresponds to the amount of body fat produced. A pound of body fat equals about 3,500 stored calories of energy. For instance, if you were to eat 7 cheeseburgers (7 cheeseburgers × 500 calories each = 3,500 calories) and not burn a single calorie of it, you would be able to produce about one pound of body fat. Of course, in real life you never save all the energy of a given food that you eat. You burn some of its energy simply in the act of chewing it, digesting it, and transporting its nutrients around your body. Yet all the calories that you do ingest and don't burn in some way or store as glycogen do get stored as body fat, at the rate of 3,500 calories per pound. Thus, you will gain weight if you eat more calories than your body uses.

Individual Differences in Forming Fat

People differ tremendously in how efficiently they convert calories into fat. Two teens could eat the exact same diet and even exercise the same amount, and one might gain weight while the other might lose it. Some people more readily burn excess calories while other people more readily store them.

In other words, many overweight teens don't eat more than their slender friends. They just have extraordinarily efficient mechanisms for storing energy. In times of starvation, such an ability could save one's life. But in times of bounty, this ability impairs rather than aids survival.

Let's now consider some of the reasons why people differ in their ability to store calories as fat. Please don't feel discouraged if some of the deck seems stacked against you. What you do will make a difference.

Genetic Factors. The genes you've inherited from your parents don't absolutely dictate whether or not you will become obese. But they do set the stage, making it either easier or harder for you to maintain normal weight. For example, among children of normal-weight parents, only about 9 percent will become obese at some point in their lives. Of children with one normal-weight parent and one obese parent (either father or mother), 41 percent are likely to become obese. Of children with two obese parents, 73 percent are likely to become obese sooner or later.

Thus, a fair number of children with slender parents become obese themselves, and more than a quarter of those children with obese parents manage to remain at normal weight throughout their lives. So don't become overly discouraged if others in your family are obese. There is no law that you must follow in their footsteps. It may take more work to remain slim, but you can do it.

Metabolism and Obesity. The metabolic rate is the speed with which you burn, or use up, the calories of energy you have consumed. Teens with a high metabolic rate tend to use more calories even in the ordinary processes of living, such as breathing and digestion of food. Teens with a low metabolic rate, on the other hand, tend to conserve calories, spending less on activity and saving more as fat. Individual differences in metabolic rate are usually determined by genetics.

There are factors besides genetics that also affect the metabolic rate, however. Some of these, such as age, gender, and height, are beyond your control. For instance, take age. Young people tend to have a higher metabolic rate than do older people. On the average, boys have a higher metabolic rate than girls. This explains the common observation that teenage boys can often eat plenty without gaining extra fat, while girls of the same age and activity levels must eat less to maintain their body weight. This means that maintaining a certain weight is tougher for girls than boys, but they can still succeed at it.

Height and body structure also affect the metabolic rate. Teens who are tall and thin for a given body weight generally have a higher metabolism and thus can eat more and still remain thin. Conversely, teens who are shorter and have stockier builds, for the same age and weight, tend to have a slower metabolism and more readily store calories.

The main factor affecting metabolism that you can control is exercise. This word scares some teens, but if you can motivate yourself into greater physical activity, it will help you lose excess weight and maintain normal weight once you reach the level that's right for you. Happily, the more you exercise the greater your metabolic rate. This means you burn calories not only during the exercise itself but even during the many hours afterward, including when resting or asleep. So exercise is the key to counterbalancing other factors such as genetics or gender that may be stacked against you. Exercise is so important that Chapter 8 is devoted solely to it.

Eating Patterns. Luckily, you can control your eating patterns, too, although it may take considerable effort to break your old, bad habits. To keep body fat down, you must reduce the intake of dietary fat. Although an excess of any major nutrient listed in Table 4 can be converted into body fat, weight gain happens much more easily with dietary fat. Why? First of all, fat contains more calories, ounce for ounce, than any other nutrient known. This makes it easier to eat an excess of calories in a fatty food such as peanuts than in a low-fat food such as carrots. Furthermore, the body can easily produce body fat from dietary fat and lose only 3 percent of the energy consumed. By contrast, the body must spend 23 percent—almost eight times as much— of the energy gained from eating carbohydrates in the chemical processes required to convert it into fat.

Eating a lot of high-fat foods makes it easier for you to gain weight. The kinds of foods high in fat that those watching their weight and health should eat less of include the following: fatty meats (such as bacon or fatty ham); high-fat dairy products such as cream, ice cream, whole milk, and regular cheese; vegetables high in oil (fat) such as avocados and nuts; and rich or creamy snacks and desserts such as chips, cakes, cookies, and pies.

You don't have to give up these foods entirely. Each one named also contains some good nutrients. Just keep consumption of fatty foods down to small amounts and/or infrequent eating. On a date at the movies, if you want a snack, eat the popcorn but skip the butter or margarine. And don't add salt, for it already contains salt. Many places nowadays offer other low-fat treats, such as low-fat ice cream or frozen yogurt.

Why We Eat. Why do you eat? Think about it for a moment. Do you know that if you eat for the wrong reasons, you could be drastically increasing your chances of becoming overweight?

Teens who eat only when they feel actual physical hunger are less likely to become obese. However, teens who eat for social and emotional reasons will quite likely pack on far more calories than they need.

What are some of these reasons? First, some teens feel they should never pass up free food, that they must always "clean their plates," or that they must eat everything someone offers them to avoid appearing rude. Also, most of us eat because we think it's "time" for a meal, whether we need to eat or not. Or we may eat due to boredom, depression, stress, or habit (for example, munching on snacks whenever watching TV). Some teens eat to soothe their anxiety or to compensate for feelings of inferiority or low self-esteem. These are the kinds of bad habits you need to start breaking. No matter how difficult that may seem at first, after the first few successful steps it gets easier.

The only *good* reason to eat is that your body needs food. Usually, therefore, if you don't feel hungry, it would be wiser not to eat, even if it's mealtime. Eating to relax, reduce stress, or "make up" for conflict and frustration in your life not only fills you with excess calories, but it may also interfere with finding more satisfying ways to resolve your problems. Furthermore, consistent overeating for psychological reasons may confuse your normal hunger-satiation system. You could lose the ability to tell when you're really hungry and when you're satiated (full), making it much harder to follow healthy eating patterns.

4

A Little Help from Your Friends:

Losing Weight with Commercial Programs and Sugar and Fat Substitutes

Many teens who are overweight don't have the time, knowledge, or motivation to design or maintain a diet on their own. They want someone to tell them just what to eat, how much to eat, and when to eat it. Or they want the encouragement of fellow dieters to help make them toe the line.

This book should provide you with all the information you need to construct a safe and healthy diet all on your own. Most of you don't really need these groups. However, if you are interested in diet organizations, a number of the most successful ones are discussed briefly in this section. Some of these groups even offer special sessions for teens.

Being included in this book does not mean that these organizations—their principles and methods—are necessarily endorsed by the author and publisher of this book. It only reflects the amount of popular attention these groups have attracted.

The wise reader will shop around carefully before joining one of these groups. Pay special attention to the relative cost as well as to how closely the groups follow the scientific principles for healthy dieting that are explained in this book. In addition, the group that is best for one person may not be best for someone else. And don't forget to check with your family doctor, who may know of special teen weight-control programs at local hospitals or clinics.

To avoid the appearance of giving preferential treatment to any particular group, they will be presented here in alphabetical order. And please realize that any of the prices or rules listed here may have changed by the time you read this.

Weight-Loss Groups

Jenny Craig. The list price for membership at a local Jenny Craig center is $185. However, special discounts are sometimes advertised. To follow the program closely, you must pay, in addition, about $60 or $70 a week for Jenny Craig food products. These special foods are required by the diet plan. At the recommended weight-loss rate of 1 to 2 pounds a week, you can calculate the number of weeks required to reach your weight-loss goal. Multiplying that number of weeks times the food cost per week will give you a pretty good idea of the total cost of the program. These products are real foods, as opposed to canned liquid or powdered diet supplements. Jenny Craig also provides a series of video classes and individual meetings with a counselor to provide nutritional and health information and emotional support.

Optifast. This plan is based on a very low calorie diet (as low as 420 calories per day) and is very costly for the full treatment. The 26-week program runs between $2,500 and $3,500 per person. One reason for the extra expense is that clients meet with physicians, registered dieticians, and other hospital professionals, not just unlicensed diet counselors. Getting such professional attention and regular instruction is a real plus for those who are extremely overweight. The program encourages weight loss of 1 to 2 percent of body weight a week, and the average weight loss is reported as 20 percent of starting weight (for example, 30 pounds for a 150-pound person). An Optifast spokesperson reports, however, that teens under the age of 18 are not generally accepted into the program.

Slim Fast/Ultra Slim Fast. This program costs about $8 to $12 per week. However, there is no instruction or supervision by licensed professionals or even corporation-trained group counselors. Each client just buys the powdered nutritional supplements and administers them privately. Without proper instruction, there is a definite potential for abuse of the product. One could grow so dependent on it that he or she forgets how to maintain weight on a diet of normal food.

Weight Watchers. This group does offer a line of diet food products. However, these products are based on real foods, not powders or liquids. And it is not essential that a client purchase them. He or she may choose any available low-calorie foods. The group does offer nutritional guidance, but the counselors have been trained within the program and usually are not licensed professionals. In addition to counselor instruction, Weight Watchers emphasizes group support. Fellow dieters are encouraged to praise each other for diet success. Another plus is the low price. The initial membership fee is usually under $20, and there are weekly dues of about $9 or less.*

*Facts about the preceding diet programs have been adapted from "Smart losers' guide to choosing a weight-loss program," *Tufts University Diet & Nutrition Letter,* August 1990, 3–6.

"Lite" Foods

To cash in on the trend toward health con-
sciousness, many food manufacturers market
lines of "lite" foods. This claim of reduced fat
and/or calories, however, is not always genuine.
Certainly, some companies have achieved a major reduction of fat in certain items. (Enten-
mann's, for example, offers a line of baked goods
that is fat-free.) However, others have accom-
plished only a very slight reduction and yet have
branded their new products as "lite." The fed-
eral government has begun planning a series of
new regulations to specify how much of a reduction in fat or calories must occur before a label such as "low-fat" or "lite" can be used. As
of this writing, it is not clear how strict these
new standards will be, but they should at least
create uniformity in the system. Meanwhile,
when in doubt, read the label of both the regular version and the "lite" version to see how
much of a difference there really is. Genuine re-
duced-fat products often cost more. But if you
find the taste and cost acceptable, such foods
can help you reduce fat and calories in food.

Some foods don't carry the label "lite," and
yet they are lighter than regular foods in one
way or another. Real butter, for example, has in
each tiny pat 35 calories, 2.5 grams of saturated
fat (the "bad" kind), and 11 milligrams of cho-

lesterol. By contrast, margarine, which is an artificial butter and contains the same number of calories in an average pat, has only 0.8 grams of saturated fat and no cholesterol at all. Similarly, each cup of ice cream typically has 270 calories, 9 grams of saturated fat, and 59 milligrams of cholesterol. But a cup of ice milk has only 185 calories, 3.5 grams of saturated fat, and 18 milligrams of cholesterol. Frozen low-fat yogurt may have as little total fat as 2 grams per cup.

Sugar Substitutes

Another way to reduce calories in food is to use substitutes for sugar. Real sugar provides 4 calories per gram (about 114 per ounce), while sugar substitutes such as saccharin and aspartame (Nutrasweet) are almost calorie-free. A regular soda, for instance, may contain about 150 calories, while one with aspartame may have only 1 or 2. Such a marked reduction suggests that sugar substitutes could make a huge impact on one's diet. However, studies of actual food consumption show that the typical person still consumes plenty of products with real sugar in addition to the sugar-free ones. In fact, the sweet taste of soda (whether filled with sugar or a sugar substitute) may actually stimulate the appetite, causing you to eat more. If you can control the impulse to gorge on real sugar, too, then the substitutes can help you cut total calories.

Fat
Substitutes

Sugar substitutes have been around for a long time, but fat substitutes are just now coming into the picture. The two main fat substitutes now in the works are called Simplesse and Olestra. Supposedly, both offer much of the same taste and feel as real fat, but for far fewer calories. Real ice cream, for instance, uses the butterfat from cream to make the product smooth and yummy. A frozen dessert with Simplesse tastes about the same but has only one or two grams of fat per cup and about half the calories of rich ice cream. Getting less fat is not only better for your waistline but also for your heart.

As good as they may sound, these new products so far have limited uses in food. Simplesse, for instance, is made from milk and egg whites but cannot be used in baking or in cooked products because heating breaks it down chemically. (Olestra, on the other hand, can be heated.) Since these products are so new, however, we don't know the possible long-term results of using them. Laboratory studies with animals show the products to be safe. But free-living humans simply don't act like rats in cages. Also, it would be possible to eat lots of fat substitutes and still eat plenty of fatty foods such as meat, whole milk, and fried foods. Teens taking that approach would not lose an ounce of body fat.

5

Risky Ways to Lose Weight: Fad Diets

Have you seen or heard ads similar to these?

**LOSE UP TO 5 POUNDS A DAY
WITHOUT EXERCISE!**

**LOSE 10 POUNDS OVERNIGHT
WHILE YOU SLEEP!**

**EAT ALL YOU WANT AND LOSE
UP TO 20 POUNDS A WEEK!**

Claims like these abound on radio and television and in magazines and newspapers. Certainly, the chance to lose lots of weight with little effort catches your attention. It sounds appealing. But what is the truth behind such claims? Are there any risks, catches, or drawbacks? How can we distinguish safe diets from dangerous ones?

What Is a
   Fad Diet?

A fad diet is an unbalanced and unhealthy diet based on little, if any, scientific justification. Rather, it is based on magical-sounding promises of terrific benefit for almost no effort. It is developed more as a money-making proposition than as a way to promote public health. A fad diet is usually first popularized in a best-selling book, gets a lot of media attention, and has a large popular following—but only for a short time. Once people try it and find that it doesn't help them lose weight, doesn't let them keep the weight off, or makes them ill, they fall off the bandwagon until the next passing fad catches the public fancy.

The Truth Behind
   Fad-Diet Claims

There are several problems with the extravagant claims made by fad diets. First of all, they never live up to their promises. Perhaps one out of a hundred or one out of a thousand people on such diets does see dramatic weight loss. But the average person sees nothing close to what he or she expects based on the marvelous claims of success that first attracted him or her.

Second, if weight loss really does occur rapidly, *it is mostly water loss rather than fat loss.* Many fad diets include pills or combinations of foods that promote *diuresis,* or increased urination. This means you excrete more body water (along with important vitamins and minerals) in the urine. Since a pint of water weighs about a pound, you can lose, say, 5 pounds of scale weight quickly by promoting the loss of 5 pints of water.

The problem is that your body needs that water! When you lose too much body water, you become partially dehydrated. Such dehydration can negatively affect your mood and mental performance. If too severe or long-term, it can damage the body's organs, including the eyes and kidneys. Therefore, your body tends to stimulate thirst to make you add the water right back on again. So you may regain the 5 pounds of weight very quickly.

Even when real fat reduction and weight loss do occur with a fad diet, the dieter almost always regains the fat, often quite quickly. The person may gain even more weight than was lost. For example, suppose you tried an unbalanced diet based primarily on fresh fruit. (Fruit is wonderful as part of a balanced diet but lacks too many important nutrients for you to live on it alone.) In a week, you might lose 3 pounds. But by then you would feel disgusted with the diet. That weekend you might binge on potato chips, ice cream, and chocolate cake—all the things you had been denying yourself for a week. As a result, you would soon gain 5 pounds, the original 3 you had struggled to lose plus 2 more!

Many fad diets also cost quite a bit of money. They may *require* you to invest in a special line of food products or to see a diet "counselor" who knows only about one diet plan and has no general background or training in medicine, health, or nutrition. Such a fad diet "counselor" is primarily a salesperson, not a genuine nutrition expert. By contrast, a good diet may offer you the option of buying special low-calorie food products but also explains how you can use ordinary whole foods. If the diet includes regularly seeing a consultant, that person will be a legitimate authority in the field of food and nutrition, perhaps a dietician, nutritionist, or even a medical doctor.

Finally, some fad diets are downright dangerous. They tend to make you weak, groggy, or temperamental. In extreme cases, serious illness and even death can result. Rapid weight loss due to an unbalanced diet not only melts away fat, it also robs your body of precious muscle protein. Vital organs such as the heart are composed largely of muscle, and protein loss can weaken the heart to the point of death long before a person loses all the fat intended. The duchess of Windsor was once quoted as saying, "You can never be too rich or too thin." But you *can* be too thin—dangerously thin.

The Differences Between Good and Bad Diets

Not all diets advertised in the media deserve scorn. Many popular diet plans do work safely and well. These good diets can be distinguished from fad diets by the realistic-sounding tone of their advertising. They appeal to common sense rather than the emotions. They stress safety and health rather than extremely rapid weight loss. They stress nutritional balance rather than some bizarre or extreme eating pattern. They promote the concept of learning to eat better for the rest of your life rather than using a magic formula that lets you retain poor eating habits while still losing weight.

An unbalanced diet will—almost from the beginning—leave you weak, sick, cranky, or feeling deprived. But a healthy diet will not only help you lose body weight, it will also leave you feeling stronger, happier, more energetic, and more alert. A good diet makes your body thrive because it provides what the body needs. A good diet makes you feel refreshed rather than drained, so you will more likely want to stick with it.

Hazards Posed by Fad Diets

There are problems associated with any form of prolonged and overly strict diet. These include irritability, anxiety or depression, confusion, and a sense of being out of touch with reality. Chronic dieters differ in the intensity of such symptoms.

In addition to such general problems, there are particular hazards connected with specific types of diets. All unbalanced fad diets can be divided into three simple categories: those too low in protein, those too low in carbohydrates, and those too low in both of these key nutrients. (A diet low in fat is good for you, unless it is so low that you find it unappetizing and can't stick with it.)

Problems Caused by Low-Protein Diets. Protein is a major building block of the body. It constitutes a large part of muscle tissue, hair, and fingernails. It forms chemical enzymes and hormones, which regulate various bodily functions. It should come as no surprise, therefore, that a deficiency in protein intake over a long time can cause problems with any of these functions. For instance, a diet low in protein can lead to muscle deterioration and weakness. It can stimulate hair loss and cause a thin, brittle look to the remaining hair. It can lower the blood pressure too much, resulting in frequent dizziness, particularly when you suddenly change position. Such diets can even help trigger gout, a painful inflammation of the joints that hinders free movement of the body.

Next time you see a fad-diet plan, ask yourself whether it provides enough protein. Do the food products recommended contain balanced protein? As a rule of thumb, teenage boys need a minimum of 0.4 grams of protein per day for each pound of body weight. Thus, a 120-pound, 15-year-old boy needs about 48 grams of protein per day (120 $\times$ 0.4 = 48). Teenage girls need about 0.36 grams of protein per day for each pound of body weight. Thus, a 110-pound, 15-year-old girl needs about 40 grams of protein per day (110 $\times$ 0.36 = 39.6). Of course, these are averages only. In general, the more physically active you are, the more protein you need. Since a quarter-pound hamburger contains 25 grams of protein and a glass of milk contains 8, the average person on a regular diet has no trouble getting enough protein. But some fad diets don't provide enough.

Problems Caused by Low-Carbohydrate Diets. Carbohydrates are the major source of bodily energy. Whether they come from simple carbohydrates (refined sugar, candy) or complex carbohydrates (starches as found in grains, vegetables, and fruits), the digestive system breaks them down into glucose, or blood sugar. The brain, in particular, requires large amounts of glucose for energy. A deficiency of carbohydrate intake, then, causes such problems as low energy, fatigue, and apathy (the feeling of not caring much about anything). It causes anxiety, nervousness, and unease. By stimulating a loss of body fluids, it can even lead to dehydration.

Problems Caused by Diets Too Low in Calories. Some fad diets provide too little of everything. The dieter doesn't get enough total calories or enough of any given nutrient. In effect, the person enters a period of voluntary self-starvation. As you might imagine, this form of fad dieting arouses the most concern. Early symptoms of a diet too low in calories include disturbed mood and irritability. If the diet continues, the person may experience muscle cramps and an increasing intolerance of cold. He or she never feels warm (except in hot weather), for the body's internal "furnace" is lacking in fuel. As muscles waste away further, the dieter may develop abnormal heartbeat rhythms. Eventually, the heart muscle may weaken to the point of death.

The kind of ultra-low calorie diet most liable to cause such a serious outcome is the type in which one shuns real food altogether and depends solely on protein drinks made of inadequately balanced protein (more common in the 1970's than now). No one should undertake such a diet on his or her own. Some of the more modern diet plans based on consuming nothing but balanced protein drinks under continuous medical supervision, however, are relatively safe. The doctor can monitor your physical condition to ensure that the diet is not going too far.

In the next chapter we will examine even more dangerous ways some teens use to control their body weight.

6

Eating Disorders

Unfortunately, eating disorders among teens are on the increase in our time. The odds are that you have one or more friends who either have one now, have had one, or will have one. Ninety percent of those with eating disorders are girls.

What Eating Disorders Are

An eating disorder is any relatively severe and long-lasting eating pattern that is abnormal and unhealthy. This includes such odd habits as the craving to eat nonfood items such as clay. But anorexia and bulimia are by far the most common teen eating disorders, and they are the only two linked closely with a fear of obesity. They are also among the most severe in their effects on health.

The Dangers
of Anorexia

The word *anorexia* literally means "without appetite." Its victims indeed act as if they have an insufficient appetite, for they eat very little and progressively lose significant amounts of weight. In fact, they lose far too much, often reaching a half-starved, emaciated appearance. However, most report feelings of tremendous hunger. They fail to eat not because of a true loss of appetite but because they have decided to severely limit their intake of food so as to rid themselves of all apparent fat.

It is important to distinguish between true anorexia and a short-term reduction in food intake. Anyone might feel reduced appetite during a period of stress or grief. Anyone might decide to lose a few pounds by cutting down on some treats for a while. Only about 1 percent of teens, most of them girls, develop true, diagnosed cases of anorexia.

True anorexia victims eat so little that they come to resemble concentration-camp victims. Teens with genuine anorexia look gaunt and emaciated, they feel extremely sensitive to cold, they're exhausted and weak, and they show signs of mental deterioration such as apathy and irritability. They sometimes suffer severe physical consequences, such as hormone imbalances that stop the young woman's menstrual cycle or cause infertility in young men. They may suffer damage in various organs such as the heart, damage that sometimes kills. In fact, about 6 percent of anorexics do die from the disorder (the pop singer Karen Carpenter, for one).

The Dangers of Bulimia

The word *bulimia* literally means "ox hunger" or "hungry as an ox." Teens with this problem act in many ways opposite to anorexics. Rather than deny themselves food, bulimics gorge freely. They pig out on all their favorite (and usually high-fat) snacks, treats, and desserts. Often, they consume thousands of calories in one session, far more than a normal meal. But this leaves them in a pickle. They may have ingested enough calories in a single sitting to add 1 to 3 pounds of body fat. What to do?

The bulimic tries to solve this problem by "undoing" the damage. She may induce vomiting, for instance, to remove the food before it can be digested. She may take laxatives in the vain hope of speeding the food through her intestinal tract before the calories can be fully absorbed. (This doesn't really work, though the resulting diarrhea and water loss may temporarily lower the scale weight.) She may take diuretics, forcing her kidneys to shed body water in the urine, thus reducing her weight on the scale but not altering her fat content one bit. Or she may slip into a strict regimen of food denial until she has worked off the extra calories. Girls in this last category may even develop anorexia. In other words, it is possible to have both eating disorders at once, swinging from one extreme of poor eating to the other.

Anyone might eat a little extra from time to time. At a wedding feast or Thanksgiving dinner, for example, anyone might eat more than planned or even more than is healthy. The normal person doesn't grow too concerned over this but just eats somewhat less over the next few meals until the calorie intake for the period balances out.

In genuine bulimia, however, the person typically binges in secret, alone, for she is ashamed of her behavior. She eats far more than normal, even more than in a normal binge. She doesn't eat balanced meals but rather snack and dessert items. Furthermore, after the binge, she doesn't moderately reduce calories until things balance out again. Rather, she takes the extreme action of a severe purge—either self-induced vomiting or abuse of laxatives or diuretics. Some experts estimate that perhaps 18 to 50 percent of young women today have had some experience with the bulimic cycle, though this number includes many who tried it only once or do it very rarely. Only a small proportion persist in the habit frequently over a long period, but no one knows how many for sure because the behavior is often kept a secret. Including the mild cases, some estimate that perhaps as many as 15 percent of teenage girls have real bulimia.

This kind of extreme behavior quite naturally has negative consequences. Drastic overeating may strain the digestive system. In rare cases, the stomach can even rupture from becoming so swollen. The purging part of the cycle is always dangerous, with the risk depending on the method used. For instance, forced vomiting may lead to severe tooth damage from the stomach acid in the vomit. The loss of digestive juices in the vomit may lead to an imbalance in body fluids that can affect the heart and kidneys. Self-induced diarrhea and excess urination can likewise throw off the chemical balance within the body. Bulimia can actually kill, though it is probably less dangerous than anorexia in that regard.

How Does One Develop an Eating Disorder?

The causes of eating disorders are not always clear. There may be genetic or biochemical factors in some cases. There may be psychological problems from early childhood or the present (such as school or family conflicts) that trigger the problem. Often, the psychological trap that immediately precedes anorexic or bulimic behavior is the double pressure to enjoy life through food and yet remain ultra-slim.

Society all around us encourages self-indulgence in food and drink as one of the main ways to enjoy life. For example, almost any popular magazine, newspaper, or TV show has ads showing attractive food that makes your mouth water at first glance. The characters in movies and TV shows are often shown indulging themselves with a bewildering array of high-fat snacks and treats. In real life, no party or ceremonial event would be complete without a table full of tasty food items. To be part of the action, to be popular, you are supposed to eat, eat, eat. . . .

But in real life most people, if they keep consuming like that, just keep putting on more and more weight. They then find themselves in conflict with another dominant pressure in society—to stay slim and trim. Models in ads—even those hawking food—and actors in shows—even those shown gorging themselves on fatty foods—are usually physically fit and quite thin.

All of these incompatible pressures put teens in a terrible bind. A person with a very high metabolism rate may be able to overeat and not gain weight. But the vast majority of us are not so lucky. (Even people in the high-metabolism category usually find their rate slowing and their weight increasing over the years.) The "solution" that some teens choose is to deny themselves all the time so as to keep temptation at bay. But soon, hunger and food boredom lead to a binge. Feeling guilty over the binge, they desperately seek a way out. For instance, they make themselves throw up or they double their resolve to eat less in the future. Over time they develop anorexia or bulimia.

Why do some teens develop eating disorders while others don't? Some experts relate the problem to childhood traumas, disturbed family relationships, chemical imbalances in the brain, or distorted self-images. But speculation about the causes often does not help much unless sufficient time is spent with a psychiatrist or psychologist to explore those causes thoroughly. Someone who already has a full-fledged eating disorder or has traumatic conflicts pushing him or her strongly toward unhealthy eating should consult a professional immediately.

Treatment of Eating Disorders

Once an eating disorder has become firmly established, there is no easy cure. Someone who's never suffered anorexia and never known an anorexic might be tempted to think, "It's simple—just tell them to eat more!"

Unfortunately, it's not that simple. Even when anorexics have been brought into the hospital and are receiving physical care, nutritional therapy, and psychiatric care, many don't improve much. Some will go to extraordinary lengths to deceive family members and doctors, pretending to change but not really doing so. Some others will begin to improve under the intense scrutiny possible in a hospital, but as soon as they are released they will go straight back to the disordered eating behavior again.

Given that treatment is difficult and that no sure cure exists, following are some of the ways professionals attempt to treat eating disorders such as anorexia and bulimia. Such procedures require expert intervention and cannot be successfully practiced on one's own.

Family Therapy. Some experts believe that eating disorders stem from an unhappy or unbalanced home life. Therefore, they meet periodically with all members of the family to try to uncover and work through the sources of conflict. They try to help the family members develop more satisfying patterns of interaction.

Individual Psychotherapy. Some victims may come from a seemingly normal family yet have deep-seated emotional or psychological problems anyway. The psychiatrist or psychologist practicing psychotherapy may spend many sessions asking probing questions and sifting through what the patient says, hoping for answers to the riddle as to why this eating disorder developed and what can be done about it.

Behavioral Modification. Some experts care little about the remote psychological roots of the problem. They focus instead on the immediate stimuli related to the disturbed eating behavior. For example, they'll have the patient keep a logbook of when the bulimic episodes occur and what might suddenly trigger them. Susan was a young sophomore in high school who often had eating binges on weekends. A few questions based on her daily logbook revealed that these episodes occurred mainly on Saturday nights when she had no date and when her parents were out for the evening. Therefore, the doctor recommended anticipating when such evenings would occur and making certain that she was not alone.

Medical Intervention. For advanced eating disorders, in addition to psychological therapies designed to overcome the problem in the future, there are often immediate medical crises to contend with. Often a doctor will prescribe intravenous feeding for an anorexic. This means that liquid food passes through a tube and needle into the patient's arm. The purpose of this is to restore healthy levels of essential nutrients as soon as possible.

Combination Therapies. Since eating disorders rarely have a single obvious cause, a combination of therapies is most often used. The patient may receive medical intervention, for example, at the same time as individual and family therapy.

With proper attention and treatment, about 60 to 80 percent of anorexic teens will recover. Even with excellent care, however, about 20 percent simply show no improvement. Many bulimic teens are never identified or seek help, but of those who do, about 90 to 100 percent show progress, cutting down their binging over time.

Prevention of Eating Disorders

Since treatment for eating disorders is difficult, the best approach is prevention. And successful prevention depends on keeping a healthy self-image and on maintaining a balanced diet.

Maintain a Healthy Self-Image. As we saw earlier, our society's obsession with thinness, together with a constant emphasis on the theme that rich food means pleasure, puts many teens in a bind. Being drawn to excessive eating on the one hand and self-denial on the other can trigger anorexia or bulimia—or both. Anorexics, in particular, seem to feel that no matter how much weight they lose, they are still too fat. When asked to draw themselves, some draw an image of a body much plumper than any mirror or photograph would show them.

Therefore, it is important for each person in our society to try to maintain a healthy and realistic self-image. Don't compare yourself with the models and actors in the media. Set your sights more realistically by comparing yourself with family and friends, if anyone. Better yet, try to find your own strengths and weaknesses without comparing yourself with others at all. In short, don't try to be someone else. Try to be the best person you can uniquely be.

Maintain a Balanced Diet. Prolonged self-denial is the typical first step toward an eating disorder. Eventually, cravings for what you've denied yourself become unbearable, and you react with either a binge or overly fierce self-control. The answer is not, of course, to indulge in all the snacks and treats you fancy. But to avoid that first step that leads to cravings, strive for a good and healthy diet, as will be detailed further in the next chapter. Such a diet is based primarily on grain products, fruits, and vegetables, with moderate amounts of meat and dairy products and with small amounts of snacks and desserts. Research demonstrates that this kind of diet leaves you more alert and energetic, with no uncontrollable cravings.

In fact, some research by Stephanie Dalvit-McPhillips[2] found that even among those who have already developed bulimia, this kind of diet can enable them to overcome the tendency to binge. She studied 28 bulimic patients for two and a half years. When chowing down their usual unbalanced diet, they indulged in frequent binges. But when operating on a good diet, they not only stopped the binges completely but even lost weight on the average.

You really can live more happily and healthily with a sound, balanced diet. Let's get into the details of how.

7

A Safe Way to Control Body Weight

You've been slaving over your homework for hours, but now it's finally over. You tuck in your notes and sock away your math book. You glance at your watch—a little time left for some fun before you have to get ready for bed. You're lying on the floor beside the phone wondering whom to call first. Then it hits you—a gnawing ache in the pit of your stomach. You had a big dinner only two hours ago, you tell yourself. You shouldn't be hungry, you say. But there it is, the hunger pangs, growing ever stronger now that you're thinking about them rather than your English paper and history assignment.

Quick, right now as you read these words, imagine yourself in the position just described. What are the first foods that you visualize? What do you do—get a snack or try to ignore your hunger?

If you're thinking about ice cream, cake, pie, cookies, candy, and other such delectables, watch out. You may not be overweight now, but if you routinely gorge on treats such as these, sooner or later you will put on fat. If you're like the average person, that fat will seem to just suddenly appear by young adulthood at the latest.

But there is something you can do about hunger pangs, whenever they occur, that won't add to your fat load. The answer to maintaining normal body weight is not denying yourself all the time. It won't help to force yourself into unbearable hunger. If anything, that's the road that leads to binges the moment your guard is down. Instead, whenever you feel hungry, go ahead and eat. That's right—this "diet" book is telling you it's okay to eat when you're hungry.

You see, the difference between putting on excess weight and keeping it off is not a matter of gorging versus starving, of enjoying life versus denying yourself, of splurging versus using self-control. It's a matter of *what* you eat, not necessarily how much. Says Jane Brody, the health columnist for *The New York Times* and a diet writer, "You have to learn to eat the right kinds of food and the calories will take care of themselves." In other words, to lose weight and keep it off you don't have to count calories all the time. You just have to learn to select the right foods to eat.

Learning to eat right is not the easiest task in the world. But even a little improvement is better than none. Start small and then make further changes later, when you feel up to them. Every improvement will help you lose excess weight and keep it off. This kind of permanent loss is what you want, not the fad-diet quick loss followed by quick regain. The techniques for both healthy weight loss and weight maintenance are really the same. These are the six key principles of a good diet:

Reduce
Fat Intake

The key to a healthy diet is to restrict fat intake. Remember, fat has more than twice the calories per ounce that protein and carbohydrates have. So, if you eat 8 ounces of a high-fat food, you'll ingest more than twice the calories as you would in 8 ounces of a low-fat food. Yet you'll probably feel no more full than if you'd chosen the low-fat way. Instead, you will have packed away all those extra calories and still want a snack or another meal just as soon afterward. If you eat that way every day, it is easy to see that you'll soon be storing excess fat at the rate of 1 pound for every 3,500 extra calories saved.

Remember also that your body converts dietary fat into body fat much more easily than it can convert other nutrients into body fat. So the extra fat you eat is more likely to show up on your scale.

So always strive to restrict fat intake. This does not mean you have to restrict total food intake, especially if you genuinely feel hungry. You need only keep fat intake down.

But that's easier said than done, isn't it? First, many types of fatty foods taste good; they add to the richness and enjoyment of a meal. Thus, the average American teen ingests between 40 and 50 percent of his or her total daily calories as fat. That's way too high. The American Heart Association and other health organizations recommend reducing fat calories to about 30 percent or less of your daily total. Luckily, you don't have to dispense with all dietary fat. Such a diet would be almost impossible to achieve in contemporary society unless you turned into a hermit and prepared all your own foods. (Keeping fat completely to zero would also be unhealthy.) Instead, just moderate your intake. You can eat anything if you take small portions or have it only on an occasional basis.

Secondly, most teens aren't fully aware of where and how much fat hides in food. You can easily see the visible fat in steak or a slice of ham. But did you know that nuts, butter, and cheese are equally or even more fatty?

No one expects you to sit down and actually total up the amount of fat you have eaten in a given day. Without having a professional dietician analyze your entire dietary intake, that would be extremely difficult. Instead, just learn to recognize the foods especially high in fat. These are itemized in further detail in Table 5. Then learn to reduce the amounts of these items in your diet. Instead, replace these foods with healthier ones, as we'll discuss in later sections. For healthy and appetizing snacks, for instance, try a whole fresh apple, low-fat yogurt, unsalted pretzels, or unbuttered popcorn.

For foods not covered here, consult the Appendix. This comprehensive list of foods gives you the calorie amounts for each standard serving. If you compare the same serving size for two different items, say steak and peas, and one has more calories, the extra calories are usually the result of fat. In other words, you don't actually need to count calories, but consult the Appendix simply to learn more about which foods are higher in calories and fat. If advised by your doctor to count calories so you can shed excess weight more quickly, you may use the Appendix to determine what serving sizes you can enjoy and still remain within your daily calorie limit. Please do not try to eat less than 1,000 to 1,200 calories per day if you are a girl or less than 1,200 to 1,500 calories per day if you are a boy unless your doctor recommends it and you are being medically supervised. Very low calorie diets can be dangerous.

TABLE 5
SOME HIGH-FAT FOODS AND
HEALTHY ALTERNATIVES

Eat Less of	*Moderate Amounts of*	*Eat More of*
Meat Items		
Cold cuts, sausage, regular hot dogs, fried meats, organ meats (e.g., liver), eggs	steak, ham, roasts, chicken or turkey hot dogs	fish, other seafood, skinless poultry
Milk Items		
Whole milk, canned milk, cream, sour cream, ice cream, butter, hard cheese, cream cheese	Low-fat milk, frozen yogurt, low-fat cheese, ice milk, margarine	skim milk, low-fat yogurt, cheese with less than 5% fat
Snacks		
Cakes, cookies, pies, candy, chips	peanut butter, unsalted peanuts, almonds, walnuts, pecans	fresh fruits, fresh veggies, unbuttered popcorn
Condiments		
Regular salad dressings, gravies, sauces, and spreads	low-fat dressings	fresh onion, garlic powder, herbs and spices

(Adapted from: *Pediatric Nutrition Highlights*. Philadelphia: Wyeth Laboratories, 1984.)

Increase Complex Carbohydrate (Starch) and Fiber Intake

About now you're probably asking yourself a couple of questions such as, if I cut down on fatty foods, what's left to eat? Plenty!

You can eat the right foods to your heart's content. Whereas a fad diet leaves you hungry most of the time, a healthy, sensible diet recognizes the validity of the hunger drive as a means of increasing your intake of essential nutrients.

The kinds of foods you can eat any time you feel hungry are those based mainly on complex carbohydrates. By contrast, the simple carbohydrates are the sugars, found heavily in candy, syrup, desserts, and other extra-sweet or overly processed items. The complex carbohydrates are those found mainly in whole, fresh foods—that is, those still in their original, farm-grown form. For instance, fresh fruits, green leafy vegetables, and legumes (beans and peas) can go straight from the farm to the store to your home without any major processing. Complex carbohydrates also include grain products such as bread, cereal, pasta, and rice, even though these usually involve more processing. (Choose whole-wheat products over white-flour ones, since they involve less processing.)

Complex carbohydrates are excellent choices for several reasons:

• They contain relatively few calories, compared with most other foods. Thus, you can eat a fairly large amount of them without consuming too many calories.

• They are tasty, without having to add extra fat or sugar. For instance, a pure, fresh apple, peach, or strawberry tastes excellent all by itself. People often add, for example, sugar and cream to strawberries. Or they'll add sugar and fat (shortening) to make apples into a pie. Of course, it may taste better to many people that way, especially if they are in the habit of eating these items. But adding those taste enhancers stacks up their calorie count. If you choose that route, you had better keep your portions small. Better yet, with practice, you could perhaps learn to appreciate the fruit by itself. Or you could add low-calorie taste enhancers such as artificial sweeteners or cinnamon. Ditto for toast and other breads—avoid excess butter and jelly. Vegetables aren't as sweet, but they each have their own distinctive flavor. With a little practice, perhaps, you can learn to enjoy most of them fresh and raw, perhaps as finger snacks or in salads with just a bit of low-fat salad dressing. Fresh lemon juice or olive oil and vinegar can also add a little zest to vegetables.

• They satisfy the hunger drive like nothing else. In the context of a balanced diet, complex carbohydrates are the foods that really fuel the body and keep your energy level high.

• They contain lots of important vitamins and minerals. You need these essential nutrients to stay healthy. The complex-carbohydrate foods such as fruits and vegetables are our main sources of such key nutrients as the B-vitamins, vitamin C, and potassium.

• They contain fiber, which is valuable for keeping the digestive tract in good shape. The insoluble fibers, for instance, help prevent constipation and colon irritability. They absorb water and add bulk to the stool, making fecal elimination easier. The soluble fibers help trap extra cholesterol and eliminate it from the body. Fruits, vegetables, and whole-grain products have plenty of both types of fiber.

Complex carbohydrates should form the mainstay of any good diet. Nutritionists estimate that you should ideally consume about 60 to 70 percent of your daily calories as complex carbohydrates.

Maintain a Balanced Diet

Moderation in all things dietary is the key to healthy, balanced nutrition. By contrast, the average teen eats way too much fat, sugar, and salt. (Unfortunately, far too many imbibe too much alcohol as well.) When shifting to a fad diet, such a person may go overboard in the other extreme, eating only fruits, for example, for some time.

Look at Table 6 for some recommended numbers of daily servings in each food group. If you can't eat that much or don't want to, that's fine. But don't eat more than what is recommended in one category just because you're eating less in another category. Eat something in each of the following categories of foods each day. (This rule does not apply to teens with food allergies or intolerance; it also does not apply to vegetarian teens.) Eat all you want in the fruit, vegetable, and grain categories, as long as you consume it without added fat and sugar. Eat up to the recommended maximum, but no more, in the meat and milk categories unless you are extremely active physically.

Improve Your Eating Habits

When you finish school, do you head for the candy and soda machines? When you get home, do you rip open a bag of cookies or potato chips as you plop in front of the TV? Habits like these

TABLE 6
SUGGESTED DAILY SERVINGS
FOR DIETARY BALANCE

Food Group	Serving Size	Portions
Fruits	whole apple, pear, etc; ½ grapefruit; melon wedge; ½ cup berries; ¾ cup juice.*	2–4
Vegetables	1 cup of leafy ones such as raw lettuce or cabbage; ½ cup for others.	3–5
Grain products (preferably whole grain)	1 slice bread; one whole roll, biscuit, or muffin; ½ bun; ½ cup cooked cereal; 1 oz of breakfast cereal.	6–11
Meat, poultry, fish, meat substitutes	1 oz meat, poultry, fish; 1 egg; ½ cup cooked, dry beans; 2 tablespoons peanut butter.	5–7**
Milk, cheese, yogurt	1 cup milk or yogurt; 1½ oz natural cheese; 2 oz processed cheese.	3–4***

*Fruit juice contains most of the same nutrients as whole fruit but lacks the fiber. Therefore, no more than half of your servings of fruit should be juice.

**The portion size for meat is set very small; instead of eating 7 different servings of an ounce each, most teens would rather have 2 servings of about a quarter-pound (4 ounces) each.

***Three servings of milk products are enough for most teens; teenage girls who are pregnant or breastfeeding need four.

(Source: *Dietary Guidelines for Americans*. Home and Garden Bulletin #232–1. Human Nutrition Information Service, April 1986.)

pile on the excess calories, and you know where those go—on the hips shortly after passing your lips. Here are some tips to cut down on the damage:

• Eat slowly, giving your brain time to catch up with your stomach and tell you when you've already had enough to eat. Taking little pauses during a meal to talk with others can help.

• When you feel hungry, eat something, even if it's just a carrot or a piece of celery. A good snack like that gives you valuable nutrients for almost no calories. It soothes your hunger before you go wild and head for the box of chocolates.

• Eat several small meals or nutritious snacks rather than one or two large meals a day. Larger meals encourage the formation of fat, while smaller meals increase the release of extra energy as body heat, even if the total number of calories eaten per day remains the same.

• Drink plenty of water with a meal and eat some high-fiber foods such as salads first. Water and fiber help you feel full without having to pack away excess calories in the process.

• Don't heap up piles of food on your plate. Instead, start with small portions on a small plate. Then go back for more only if you still feel really hungry. Never feel like you must "clean your plate," whether hungry or not. It's better to save or even toss out extra food than turn it into fat around your ribs.

• If you grocery shop for your family, do it on a full stomach. It's easier to spurn enticing junk foods. At home, keep problem foods out of sight and leave healthy foods visible and handy. If you do eat junk food, do so only in small amounts and only occasionally, perhaps after a healthy meal or as a special treat.

• Reduce the amount of condiments you add to food. Items such as mayonnaise and catsup add lots of calories and salt that you really don't need. Often they mask rather than enhance the true flavors of food. If you really like them, you don't have to do without completely. But reduce the frequency and amount to the least you can get by with and still enjoy your food.

• Eat in one place, not all over the house, in front of the TV, or while on the phone. Eating during other activities builds the habit of eating when you engage in those activities again, even if you're not hungry.

• If you know you're going to a party, social function, or restaurant, plan in advance what you'll do. Allow yourself some treats, but decide on your limits before you get carried away looking at the food table or dessert tray.

• Reward yourself for dietary improvements, but not with food rewards. Instead, give yourself a pat on the back, let a friend or a family member praise you, call your best friend on the phone for a chat, go to the mall, buy yourself something special you've been wanting, or do anything else you find special and enjoyable. Such rewards make sticking to your diet a lot easier.

• Get your friends and family to help. Make sure they won't tempt you with foods you're trying to avoid. Danny Wood, of the rock group The New Kids on the Block, is called "the food cop" by the other fellows in the group. Not only is he concerned about his own health, but he encourages his buddies to avoid junk and eat the right foods instead. One of fellow singer Jordan Knight's favorite drinks is chocolate milkshakes (about 400 calories each). Danny prefers water. His example helps show the others a better way.

• Avoid yo-yo dieting, periods of food restriction followed by gluttony. Instead, gradually try to improve your diet and see whether you can stick with that change permanently. One or two long-term changes are better than a dozen temporary ones.

• Never lose sight of the purpose of all your efforts. To keep motivation high, write down your weight-loss and behavioral-change goals and remind yourself of them daily.

• Don't collapse over a relapse. Don't condemn yourself for an occasional splurge beyond what you had planned. An occasional extra treat won't derail your program. Guilt and worry only make it more likely that you'll overeat again. Instead, just calmly get back to your program.

• Avoid negative thinking. Just shut your mind to thoughts such as the following: "I'm no good," "I'll never make it," "I don't have what it takes," etc. Replace such thoughts with restatements of your goal or by turning negatives into positives. For example, instead of "I'll never make it," reverse that thought into "I *will* make it."

Understand Your Eating Tendencies

Sometimes simply changing eating behavior is not enough. The pressures that led to poor eating habits are still there. For example, if you eat from boredom, spend time examining your life to determine why you feel bored. Can you think of other activities besides eating that could relieve the boredom?

If you eat to compensate for a sense of inferiority, start to examine why you feel inferior and what you can do about it. Talk to parents, friends, a favorite teacher, or a counselor at school. Perhaps you could begin a program of self-affirmation in which you identify and dwell on your strengths rather than your weaknesses. You could select activities that allow you to meet more people or give you a greater opportunity to excel so that praise, recognition, or a sense of achievement can boost your ego.

Understanding yourself better helps you improve not only your diet but your whole life. If it seems that you are unable to work through these issues on your own, then don't be afraid to seek the help of a professional. Ask your school guidance counselor or a trusted relative for a suggestion.

Developing self-understanding is tough work. It takes time, but it can be done.

Get Enough Water

Do you think you get enough to drink? Unless you take special care to, you might not. Many people wander frequently in and out of a slightly dehydrated state. Mild dehydration tends to dampen your mental sharpness, sense of well-being, and physical prowess. Even a 2 percent level of dehydration can reduce work capacity by 10 to 15 percent. More extreme cases can cause organ damage; really serious cases of dehydration can even kill.

Why don't we drink enough? The thirst drive often misses the mark. Particularly in warm weather or when exercising, you can quickly lose several pints of water through perspiration and air breathed through your moistened lungs. You can actually become fairly dehydrated in a short while without being aware of it. You may drink only a little and think you've had enough when you really haven't.

You should drink at least eight glasses of fluids a day, more when the weather is hot or you've been exercising. And don't wait for thirst to tell you to drink. Instead, drink in anticipation of thirst. Drink a little more than you think you need. The best sign that you've truly had enough water is that your urine is light and clear rather than dark. (Note: Some vitamin pills and certain medications add color to your urine temporarily, but this should not affect your level of dehydration at all.)

And while making sure you're drinking enough, consider drinking just plain water. Many young people never seem to touch the stuff. Whenever thirsty, they pop open a can of soda or grab a glass of milk or juice. Such beverages have their place, and they certainly can enhance a meal. But relying on them exclusively for fluid intake adds unneeded calories (and cost) to the diet. For instance, a can of regular soda has 150 or more calories. A cup of whole milk also has about 150, and skim milk has 85. A cup of juice adds 100 to 125, depending on the type. Plain coffee or tea has very few calories, but every tablespoon of sugar adds 45, and every tablespoon of cream adds about 30 more. Diet soda has only one or two calories per can, so that won't up your calorie intake directly. But many people find that the sweet taste of diet soda—or any other sweetened beverage—increases their appetite for snack foods, which do contain calories.

So if you're drinking just to quench thirst or ensure adequate hydration, learn to rely more on plain water.

Is Dieting Really for Teens?

Yes, if you are seriously overweight. One very comprehensive study[3] found that some diet patterns worked much better than others, however. This study examined 11 boys and 36 girls who were all obese. They averaged more than 40 percent overweight and ranged in age from 9 to 18. For 12 weeks they were administered one of five different diet plans, some of which included hints on improving eating behavior.

Others allowed dieters sticking to the diet plan to earn points for such treats as television time. At the end of one year the differences were examined.

The results in a study such as this one are complicated by the fact that preteens and young teens are still growing. Losing fat for teens does not necessarily (though it may) require losing weight. The person's weight may stay the same or even go up slightly, as he or she adds bone and muscle weight, while actually losing flab and growing more slender. So as a comparison, one group of these children received no dietary treatment (this is called having a "control group"), and they gained an average of 18 pounds over the year of the study.

In contrast to the control group's rather large weight gain, a diet group that got no reward for sticking to the diet plan gained 9.5 pounds, while a diet group allowed to reward themselves gained 7.7 pounds. The diet group that could reward themselves and also received behavioral change hints such as those described earlier in this chapter gained only 1.6 pounds. Finally, the best results were obtained by the group that didn't focus on rewards but did emphasize changing their behavior. This group actually lost an average of −0.3 pounds, which is quite an improvement over the control group's gain of 18 pounds.

In short, behavioral change and a healthy diet really work! The approach outlined in this book can help you lose excess weight and keep it off. There is just one more secret ingredient needed, and for that you must turn the page.

8

The Secret Formula for Controlling Weight: Exercise

Please Don't Stop Reading

If the word "exercise" scares you, and you're tempted to skip this chapter, please resist the temptation. Exercise does not just refer to some of the more boring or strenuous stuff you've endured in PE classes. It doesn't just mean standing in formation and proceeding in a regimented style through a bunch of boring calisthenics. It doesn't necessarily imply team sports.

The definition of exercise this author likes best is anything that involves moving your body around and that you enjoy doing. If you like aerobic dancing or following an instructor in a TV exercise show, fine. If you like a vigorous game of squash or racquetball, that's great. But if you don't like organized group and team activities, think about swimming, riding a bike, or just plain walking. Many teens get all the exercise they need just walking or riding their bikes to school.

The key to getting started is finding something *you* like to do—not something your parents, teacher, or Aunt Martha thinks you should do. What do *you* want to do that's physically active? So pick your thing, but pick *something*. Successful people realize they must keep physically active to remain healthy and stay on top. Reportedly, Madonna spends about four hours every day in exercise, doing everything from swimming and running to calisthenics. You don't have to get that active to stay slim and healthy, but do something. As one sports-shoe advertisement says, "Just do it!"

Aerobic
Exercise

Even activities such as shopping and gardening count as exercise and have value. But to get the maximum weight loss and health benefits out of your exercise, there are certain intensity levels you will want to reach, at least some of the time. When you do aerobic exercise, your heart and pulse rates will rise to somewhere in the range of 120 to 150 beats a minute. You should try to do aerobic exercise at least three times a week for at least 20 to 30 minutes each time. More sedate activities such as strolling through the woods or idling in the pool are great for the rest of the week, but do try to get more active at least this often. It only adds up to about an hour and a half per week out of a 168-hour week. That's not much of a time commitment, if you can just get serious about starting and sticking with exercise.

But let's face it. A lot of teens find it hard to maintain an exercise program. To overcome your natural resistance, it pays to become fully informed about the health benefits of aerobic exercise. Then decide what your best exercise options are. Try making a contract with yourself that you'll stick to the plan. For instance, you might write down and put up on your bulletin board, "In order to achieve my goal of keeping slender and healthy, I pledge to ride my bike for 30 minutes each day on Monday, Wednesday, and Friday. Signed: _____."

Extensive research has shown that a regular program of even three short periods of aerobic exercise per week has an incredible variety of health benefits. First of all, it strengthens the heart and lungs, two organs essential for life. It adds to the average lifespan. It helps you lose or maintain body weight (more on this soon). It makes you look and feel better. It eases stress and provides you with a psychological and emotional lift. It should come as no surprise that a study done by Paffenbarger[4] for a number of years on 16,936 Harvard graduates found amazingly beneficial effects of exercise. Those who used 2,000 or more calories per week in exercise had a death rate one-third lower than those who didn't exercise at all.

How Exercise Helps With Weight Loss

All exercises, even the more leisurely forms, burn calories you've consumed in your diet. If you're eating less than you use, then exercise starts burning up the calories in the fat you've already stored. As we saw before, each pound of fat represents 3,500 stored calories of energy. How much exercise does it take to burn off a pound of fat, then?

As a general rule of thumb, you spend about 100 calories per mile whether walking, jogging, or running. For other activities, consult Table 7 on the next page.

If you compare this table of caloric expenditures with the tables of how many calories are found in food (see the Appendix), you can actually calculate how much exercise it takes to burn off the calories in a given food you've eaten. For

TABLE 7
COMMON ACTIVITIES AND THE
CALORIES THEY BURN

Activity	Calories Spent per Hour
Lying quietly*	80–100
Sitting quietly	85–105
Standing quietly	100–120
Walking slowly (24 min/mile)	210–230
Walking quickly (15 min/mile)	315–345
Light work (cleaning house, home-work, shopping)	125–310
Moderate work (cycling at 9 mph, jogging at 6 mph, tennis, scrubbing floors, weeding garden)	315–480
Heavy work (aerobic dancing, basket-ball, chopping wood, cross-country skiing, running at 7 mph, shoveling snow, spading garden, swimming)	480–625

*Lying quietly is not an exercise, but the body still burns calories to maintain its internal activities and vital life processes (metabolism). The difference between this baseline level of caloric expenditure and that of the other activities reflects how many additional calories over basic metabolism such activities require.

(Source: *Dietary Guidelines for Americans: Maintain Desirable Weight*. Home and Garden Bulletin #232–2. Human Nutrition Information Service, April 1986, p. 8.)

example, a slice of apple pie contains about 345 calories, and that would take an hour of quick walking to work off. But a snack of a raw carrot has only 20 calories, and you could work that off with less than 4 minutes of quick walking.

As we said earlier, not only does vigorous aerobic exercise burn calories during the activity, it also raises your overall metabolic rate for several hours afterward. This allows you to burn more calories even when resting or sleeping than you would have otherwise.

Since exercise makes you burn calories, you might think it would drastically increase the appetite and make you eat so much more that you wouldn't lose weight. But this is not what happens. Moderate exercise helps you control your appetite. Since you feel so much happier and better after a workout, you find you don't need the comfort of rich and sweet treats so much.

Exercise also helps ensure that body fat rather than muscle is lost during dieting. A typical fad dieter who doesn't exercise loses body muscle as well as fat. Then, when the person gets off the fad diet and regains weight, he or she usually adds back mostly fat. So an unbalanced fad diet can leave you actually fatter afterward than you were before. But regular exercise, particularly when combined with a balanced diet, helps preserve muscle and ensure that mostly fat gets burned to provide the calories you need.

How to Start a
Regular Exercise Program

Be sure to consult your family doctor before starting any new diet or exercise program, particularly if you are seriously overweight or have any sort of health problem.

Once your doctor has cleared you for exercise, make sure you don't try to do too much too soon. Take your time and try to build up gradually. You want to develop a comfortable exercise pattern that you enjoy and can live with for a long time. Don't try to keep breaking distance or speed records or whatever (unless you're on a school team), for you may injure yourself. And you will also probably burn out and quit your exercise program altogether.

If you do get an exercise-related injury, please take care of it and either stop exercising or lessen its frequency and intensity until you are fully healed. Otherwise, you might turn a simple acute injury into a chronic pain that plagues you for years.

Many teens don't need to exercise on their own because they are involved with team sports in school. If you play football, basketball, or soccer, if you run track or engage in any other sport that keeps you moving, then you probably get enough exercise already.

Many other teens don't like to exercise on their own. Either they want to work out with friends, or they like to do it in synch with TV exercise shows or videotapes. There are a number of good ones to choose from. Just be careful not to imitate moves you're not yet ready for, especially with the so-called "high-impact" aerobics.

Many out-of-shape teens have made the mistake of assuming they could immediately do what Jane Fonda does on her videotapes. But rather than improve their health, they tear muscles or rip tendons. Flexibility and strength conditioning take time. If you keep at it, eventually you will be able to safely stretch and bounce around like Fonda.

Sticking With It

We all tend to make lots of resolutions for self-improvement and then break them. This happens most often when we try to change too much too fast. To help get your exercise program started and to stick with it:

• Remind yourself of your exercise goals every day. Post your exercise "contract" beside your bedroom mirror or some other place where you'll see it frequently. Reread it at least once a day.

• Schedule your exercise periods in advance, and don't let any interruptions stop them.

• Unless you're a serious athletic competitor, forget the slogan "No pain, no gain." Instead, try to choose enjoyable activities and do them only for the time and to the extent that they remain enjoyable.

• If you sustain an injury, take care of it and stop the activity that caused it. Try another activity if it doesn't affect your injured site. (For instance, if you develop tennis elbow, stop tennis for a while and go for walks instead.) Once you've recovered, get back into your preferred activity gradually, to ensure you don't re-injure yourself.

A Final Word

Remember, just let exercise be as much fun as you can make it (realizing it may not *always* feel like fun and sometimes may even feel like plain hard work), and then you'll be willing to stick with it. You'll enjoy each day a little more. A good diet and exercise not only add more years to your life but more life to your years. So don't just sit on your duff. Get cleared by your family physician and get out there and get involved. No one else can do it for you. But you can, and soon you'll see a more vibrant, slender, and healthier you looking proudly back from the mirror.

9

Some Final
Questions and Answers
About Diet

How do you beat the
pizza parlor dilemma?

Your crowd and the date you're with want to go
to the pizza parlor after the movie. You're trying
to lose weight, but you don't want to seem like
a health nut or party pooper around your friends.
What do you do?

You can go with them and still watch your
diet.

Look for the lower calorie entries on the
menu and order those without making an issue
of what you're up to. Drink water, sugarless iced
tea, or at least diet soda rather than regular. Ask
for thick crust pizza if you can (the extra bread
fills you up for less calories than more cheese).
Avoid most meat toppings and choose vegetable
toppings instead. If there is a salad bar, take very
small amounts of items full of mayonnaise (such

as potato salad or macaroni salad) or oil (three-bean salad, for example). Keep dressing on your salad to a minimum. You can have fun on your date, eat hundreds of fewer calories than your friends, and no one will even notice.

Are fast foods unhealthy?

There is no simple answer to this question. The main thing to watch out for with any food, fast or not, is the fat. At a typical burger place you can avoid most fat if you really try, but it is not easy. For example, a diet soda and a fresh salad without dressing would make a low-fat lunch (see Table 8). Adding croutons, bacon bits, and salad dressing, however, quickly multiplies the fat by three and the calories by five. All the meat items have fat to begin with, while all the deep-fried items absorb extra fat from the animal or vegetable shortening used in the frying process. A plain baked potato, for instance, has almost no fat, whereas the french-frying process adds loads of fat. Compare the items in Table 8 to find the best fat and calorie bargains.

Does Table 8 mean you can never eat a cheeseburger or fries? Of course not. Even high-fat items may be consumed occasionally, as long as you don't make a habit of it and stay physically active enough.

TABLE 8
TOTAL CALORIES AND FAT
IN COMMON FAST FOODS

Item	Calories per Serving	Grams of Fat
Arby's roast beef sandwich	350 cal	15 g
Arthur Treacher's fried fish	350	20
Burger King whopper with cheese	740	45
Burger King chocolate shake	340	10
Kentucky-Fried chicken breast	200	12
McDonald's Egg McMuffin	290	11
McDonald's garden salad (plain)	110	7
McDonald's salad with croutons, bacon bits, and 1 package of Ranch dressing	506	19
McDonald's McLean Sandwich	320	10
Taco Bell taco	162	9
Wendy's french fries	330	16
Wendy's regular hamburger	470	26

(Sources: Zimmer, J., and Aaron, R. *The Fat Gram Counter.* New York: Berkley Books, 1986. And *McDonald's Food: The Facts,* 1990.)

Can diet
cure acne?

Acne is one problem confronted sooner or later by most teens. Whether you have a mild or severe case depends mostly on your genetic background, your hormones (which affect oil production), the cleanliness of your environment, and how well you care for your skin. Some teens find that stress and tension make their problem worse. Despite what you may have heard, diet and acne are not related. It's only a myth that certain foods such as chocolate make you break out while other foods can clear you up. Even if it won't cure acne, however, a low-fat, balanced diet will help keep you healthier, slimmer, and happier in other ways. If your acne problem is serious, see a dermatologist, who has an arsenal of new therapies that can be of great help.

What should you eat to help athletic performance?

Don't make the mistake of thinking that, because muscles are built from protein, you must emphasize protein in your diet to build larger muscles. The average teen consumes, if anything, too much protein. The balanced diet prescribed in this book provides all the nutrients needed to keep the average athlete in good shape. However, the athlete who regularly engages in vigorous exercise may need more total calories than the usual recommendation. This supplement should come from complex carbohydrates (fruits, vegetables, and whole-grain products) rather than high-protein (and usually high-fat) foods. The athlete needs more energy, not protein, in this case.

Some athletes believe in eating special foods just before participating in an event. When this author ran the mile on the high school track team, for instance, the coach taught that we should slurp plain honey just before stepping into the starting blocks. We now recognize that it is better to eat nothing just before an event. Any food in your stomach when you're working out detours blood from the muscles where it's needed most during the event. The best approach is to get plenty of complex carbohydrates in the meal preceding the game or contest, but eat nothing 2 to 4 hours just before it starts. Do drink plenty of water to avoid dehydration, but avoid sugary beverages.

Is it okay to lose weight rapidly?

Many teens practice last minute, panic dieting. Some athletes, such as wrestlers, want to get into a lower weight category. Some teen girls want to fit into a special outfit or a new swimsuit. To lose weight rapidly, however, is unhealthy, particularly if you use drugs such as diuretics (to promote water loss) or amphetamines (to reduce appetite). Even if you lose the weight you want, the odds are you won't feel as well as normal, and thus will not enjoy the event you're going to. And the weight will usually bounce right back on. Forget the idea of quick dieting for a limited purpose followed by slipping back into your old eating patterns. It's better to reorganize your whole approach to food and develop healthier eating habits you can live with always. That will help you keep the fat level down permanently.

If it's not cool to diet in your crowd, what can you do?

In many school lunchrooms, only the girls use the salad bar. Many of the boys who want to eat healthier or diet are too shy to get a salad. No one wants to be teased or looked down on, but that shouldn't happen just because you pick salad over a greasy cheeseburger. Just don't make an issue of why you've chosen greens. If you nag others about eating too much fat, they may tease you just as a way of getting you off their backs. If you do choose a healthy item and someone asks you about it, you can always say "it tastes great" or "I like it" rather than confess to dieting. They'll respect you for living by your food choices if you, in turn, respect them.

What if a parent or friend pressures you to keep eating?

If it's parents, explain to them that you're trying to watch calories and feel you've had enough to eat. If your diet is balanced, but just light in total volume, they shouldn't worry. (A parent will worry about anorexia if you eat a severely unbalanced diet or are becoming gaunt. That's different.)

A host at a party means for you to have a good time. Some urge their treats on you more than they should, but they mean well. Just say something like, "I've really enjoyed it—it's great. But I've had enough. Thank you." If pressure continues, say you'd rather have fruit or more coffee (or whatever other low-cal item is available) than another piece of cheesecake (or whatever other rich treat they're pushing). Then stick to your guns. Just keep a polite smile, and you can remain a model guest while still watching your diet.

Do any healthy snacks taste good?

There are two ways to solve the problem many young people have of preferring high-fat foods to those they know are healthy for them. First, you can keep trying healthy foods until you find those you like best. The more you try them, the better you'll like certain ones. For instance, the first time you try plain carrot or celery sticks you may find them barely acceptable as snacks. But after trying them several times, you may be pleased to find that they grow on you, especially when you realize how much better you feel after eating them rather than cookies and candy. Maybe you'll discover you like fresh vegetables better with just a bit of low-calorie salad dressing or dip. You could try a sprinkle of lemon juice or a spice such as pepper or curry powder to jazz them up. Get inventive, and you'll find something you like or can at least tolerate. Here are some truly healthy snacks:

- Broccoli and cauliflower chunks
- Fresh tomato slices or cherry tomatoes
- Any other salad vegetable except avocados (too high in fat)
- A fresh apple, banana, orange, pear, or other fruit
- Whole-grain muffins or biscuits (without butter and jelly)
- Whole-grain toast with or without a sprinkle of cinnamon
- Unbuttered popcorn
- Low-fat yogurt

If you really don't like any of these healthy foods as snacks, the second approach is to select items you do like, but pick the ones lowest in oil or other fats, sugar, and salt. Here are some ideas for snacks that are better than other alternatives in the same category.

- Cake   angel food without frosting
- Candy   jelly beans, gummi bears and other gumlike candies, lollipops
- Chips   pretzels
- Cookies   vanilla wafers, gingersnaps
- Gum   those sweetened with xylitol rather than sucrose
- Ice cream low-fat frozen yogurt, sherbet
- Soda   any with aspartame rather than sugar; preferably without caffeine

Is sugar bad for you?

Yes and no. Sort of. Well, maybe. The answers to this question keep changing depending on which authority you consult. The bad side: repeated exposure to sugar (whether in candy or any other sweet treat) encourages tooth decay.

Eating a lot of sugary treats adds to your total calorie load, and this can add body fat or displace more healthful foods from your diet. Excess sugar can throw off your moods and make you drowsy. If you're hungry and munch only on a sweet treat, you might get a brief sugar-induced arousal, but that will be followed by a longer period of lethargy. The okay side: practically everyone has a sweet tooth, and sugar can make foods more enjoyable. Other than among diabetics, it appears to have no harmful effects on the body as long as the total intake does not exceed about 5 to 15 percent of your daily calories. For example, that's 100 to 300 calories out of a 2,000-calorie-per-day intake. Sugar is safest when consumed as part of a well-balanced meal rather than by itself.

Do you have to starve to stay thin?

No. Skipping meals, depriving yourself of all your favorite foods, and severely restricting total intake (unless recommended to do so by your doctor) may lead to eating disorders or make you ill. Such self-punitive behaviors probably will not help you keep weight down in the long run. Instead, self-starvation leads to cycles of weight loss and gain, often to new weight highs each time. Healthy, balanced, modest eating is the best way both to lose weight and to keep it off. The normal person really needn't separate weight loss from weight maintenance. Practicing healthy eating habits will achieve both goals.

Appendix: A Table of Common Foods and the Calories They Contain

This appendix contains a list of food categories (fruits, vegetables, meat, etc.), some key foods in each category, standard portion sizes of each, and the calories in each portion. This is not meant to encourage counting of calories, but to indicate which foods are less calorie-dense. Foods with lots of calories for the same portion size generally are high in fat and should be consumed less often. Foods with few calories for the same portion size usually have more fiber and complex carbohydrates and should be consumed more often. (Source: *Food and Your Weight.* Home and Garden Bulletin #74. Updated. U.S. Department of Agriculture, 1967.) Please note that calorie counts for fast-food meals can be found on p. 108.

MILK, CHEESE, AND ICE CREAM

Fluid milk:		*cals.*
Whole	1 cup or glass	160
2% milk	1 cup	125
1% milk	1 cup	105
Skim (fresh or nonfat dry reconstituted)	1 cup or glass	90

Buttermilk	1 cup or glass	90
Evaporated (undiluted)	½ cup	170
Condensed, sweetened (undiluted)	½ cup	490
Half-and-half	1 cup	325
(milk and cream)	1 tablespoon	20
Soymilk	1 cup	50
Cream, light	1 tablespoon	30
Cream, heavy whipping	1 tablespoon	55
Yogurt (made from partially skimmed milk)	1 cup	120
Cheese:		
American, cheddar-type	1 ounce	115
	1-inch cube (⅗ ounce)	70
	½ cup, grated (2 ounces)	225
Process American, cheddar-type	1 ounce	105
Blue-mold (or Roquefort-type)	1 ounce	105
Cottage, not creamed	2 tablespoons (1 ounce)	25
Cottage, creamed	2 tablespoons (1 ounce)	30
Cream	2 tablespoons (1 ounce)	105
Parmesan, dry, grated	2 tablespoons (⅓ ounce)	40
Swiss	1 ounce	105
Milk beverages:		
Cocoa (all milk)	1 cup	235
Chocolate-flavored milk drink	1 cup	190
Malted milk	1 cup	280
Chocolate milkshake	One 12-ounce container	520
Ice cream, plain	1 container (3½ fluid ounces)	130
Ice milk	½ cup (4 fluid ounces)	140
Ice cream soda, chocolate	1 large glass	455
Frozen yogurt, plain	1 cup	145
Frozen yogurt, fruited	1 cup	230

MEAT, POULTRY, FISH, EGGS, DRY BEANS AND PEAS, NUTS

Meat, cooked, without bone: *cals.*
Beef:
  Pot roast or braised:

Lean and fat	3 ounces	245
	(1 thick or 2 thin slices, 4 by 2½ inches)	
Lean only	2½ ounces	140
	(1 thick or 2 thin slices, 4 by 2 inches)	

  Oven roast
  (relatively large
  proportion of fat
  to lean):

Lean and fat	3 ounces	375
	(1 thick or 2 thin slices, 4 by 2½ inches)	
Lean only	2 ounces	140
	(1 thick or 2 thin slices, 4 by 1½ inches)	

  Oven roast
  (relatively low
  proportion of fat
  to lean):

Lean and fat	3 ounces	165
	(1 thick or 2 thin slices, 4 by 2½ inches)	
Lean only	2½ ounces	115
	(1 thick or 2 thin slices, 4 by 2 inches)	

  Steak, broiled:

Lean and fat	3 ounces (1 piece, 4 by 2½ inches by ½ inch)	330
Lean only	2 ounces (1 piece, 4 by 1½ inches by ½ inch)	115

Hamburger patty:		
Regular ground beef	3-ounce patty (about 4 patties per pound of raw meat)	245
Lean ground round	3-ounce patty (about 4 patties per pound of raw meat)	185
Corned beef, canned	3 ounces (1 piece, 4 by 2½ inches by ½ inch)	185
Corned beef hash, canned	3 ounces (scant half cup)	155
Meat loaf	2 ounces (1 piece, 4 by 2½ inches by ½ inch)	115
Beef and vegetable stew	½ cup	105
Beef potpie, baked	1 pie, 4¼ inch diameter, about 8 ounces before baking	560
Chile con carne, canned:		
Without beans	½ cup	255
With beans	½ cup	170
Veal:		
Cutlet, broiled, meat only	3 ounces (1 cutlet, 4 by 2½ inches by ½ inch)	185
Lamb:		
Chop (about 2½ chops to a pound, as purchased)		
Lean and fat	4 ounces	400
Lean only	2⅗ ounces	140
Roast, leg:		
Lean and fat	3 ounces (1 thick or 2 thin slices, 3½ by 3 inches)	235
Lean only	2½ ounces (1 thick or 2 thin slices, 3½ by 2½ inches)	130

Pork:

Chop (about 3 chops
to a pound, as pur-
chased)

Lean and fat	2⅓ ounces	260
Lean only	2 ounces	155

Roast, loin:

Lean and fat	3 ounces (1 thick or 2 thin slices, 4 by 2½ inches)	310
Lean only	2⅖ ounces (1 thick or 2 thin slices, 3 by 2½ inches)	175

Cured Ham:

Lean and fat	3 ounces (1 thick or 2 thin slices, 4 by 2 inches)	245
Lean only	2⅕ ounces (1 thick or 2 thin slices, 3½ by 2 inches)	120

Bacon, broiled or fried	2 very thin slices	100

Sausage and luncheon
meats:

Bologna sausage	2 ounces (2 very thin slices, 4 inches in diameter)	170
Liver sausage (liver- wurst)	2 ounces (4 very thin slices, 3 inches in diameter)	175
Vienna sausage, canned	2 ounces (4 to 5 sausages)	135
Pork sausage, bulk	2 ounces (1 patty, 2 inches in diameter; 4 to 5 patties per pound of raw meat)	270
Liver, beef, fried (in- cludes fat for frying)	2 ounces (1 thick piece, 3 by 2½ inches)	130
Tongue, beef, braised	3 ounces (1 thick slice, 4 by 2½ inches)	210

Frankfurter	1 frankfurter	155
Boiled ham (luncheon meat)	2 ounces (2 very thin slices, 3½ by 3½ inches)	135
Spiced ham, canned	2 ounces (2 thin slices, 3 by 2½ inches)	165
Poultry, cooked, without bone:		
Chicken:		
Broiled	3 ounces (about ¼ of a small broiler)	185
Fried	½ breast, 2⅘ ounces	155
	1 leg (thigh and drumstick), 3 ounces	225
Canned	3½ ounces (½ cup)	200
Chicken nuggets	6 pieces	290
Poultry pie (with potatoes, peas, and gravy)	1 small pie, 4¼ inches in diameter (about 8 ounces before cooking)	535
Turkey bologna	1 slice	55
Fish and shellfish:		
Bluefish, baked	3 ounces (1 piece, 3½ by 2 inches by ½ inch)	135
Clams, shelled:		
Raw, meat only	3 ounces (about 4 medium clams)	65
Canned, clams and juice	3 ounces (1 scant half cup, 3 medium clams and juice)	45
Crab meat, canned or cooked	3 ounces, ½ cup	85
Fish sticks, breaded, cooked, frozen (including breading and fat for frying)	4 ounces (5 fish sticks)	200
Mackerel:		
Broiled	3 ounces (1 piece, 4 by 3 inches by ½ inch)	200
Canned	3 ounces, solids and liquid (about ⅗ cup)	155

Ocean perch, fried (including egg, breadcrumbs, and fat for frying)	3 ounces (1 piece, 4 by 2½ inches by ½ inch)	195
Oysters, shucked: raw, meat only	½ cup (6 to 10 medium-size oysters, selects)	80
Salmon:		
Broiled or baked	4 ounces (1 steak, 4½ by 2½ inches by ½ inch)	205
Canned (pink)	3 ounces, solids and liquid, about ⅗ cup	120
Sardines, canned in oil	3 ounces, drained solids (5 to 7 medium sardines)	175
Shrimp, canned, meat only	3 ounces (about 17 medium shrimp)	100
Tunafish, canned in oil, meat only	3 ounces (about ⅖ cup)	170
Tunafish, canned in water, meat only	3 ounces	110
Eggs:		
Fried (including fat for frying)	1 large egg	100
Hard or soft cooked, "boiled"	1 large egg	80
Scrambled or omelet (including milk and fat for cooking)	1 large egg	110
Poached	1 large egg	80
Dry beans and peas:		
Red kidney beans, canned or cooked	½ cup, solids and liquid	115
Lima, cooked	½ cup, solids and liquid	130
Baked beans, with tomato or molasses:		
With pork	½ cup	160
Without pork	½ cup	155

Nuts:

Almonds, shelled	2 tablespoons (about 13 to 15 almonds)	105
Brazil nuts, shelled	2 tablespoons	115
Cashew nuts, roasted	2 tablespoons (about 4 to 5 nuts)	95
Coconut:		
Fresh, shredded meat	2 tablespoons	40
Dried, shredded, sweetened	2 tablespoons	45
Peanuts, roasted, shelled	2 tablespoons	105
Peanut butter	1 tablespoon	95
Pecans, shelled halves	2 tablespoons (about 12 to 14 halves)	95
Walnuts, shelled:		
Black or native, chopped	2 tablespoons	100
English or Persian, halves	2 tablespoons (about 7 to 12 halves)	80

VEGETABLES AND FRUITS

Vegetables:		*cals.*
Asparagus, cooked or canned	6 medium spears or ½ cup cut spears	20
Beans:		
Lima, green, cooked or canned	½ cup	80
Snap, green, wax or yellow, cooked or canned	½ cup	15
Beets, cooked or canned	½ cup, diced	30
Beet greens, cooked	½ cup	15
Broccoli, cooked	½ cup flower stalks	20
Brussels sprouts, cooked	½ cup	20

Cabbage:		
Raw	½ cup, shredded	10
	1 wedge, 3½ by 4½ inches	25
Coleslaw (with mayonnaise-type salad dressing)	½ cup	60
Cooked	½ cup	20
Carrots:		
Raw	1 carrot, 5½ inches by 1 inch in diameter, or 25 thin slices	20
	½ cup, grated	20
Cooked	½ cup, diced	20
Cauliflower, cooked	½ cup flower buds	10
Celery, raw	2 large stalks, 8 inches long, or 3 small stalks, 5 inches long	10
Collards, cooked	½ cup	30
Corn:		
On cob, cooked	1 ear, 5 inches long	70
Kernels, cooked or canned	½ cup	85
Cucumbers, raw, pared	6 slices, ⅛ inch thick, center section	5
Kale, cooked	½ cup	15
Lettuce, raw	2 large or 4 small leaves	10
Mushrooms, canned	½ cup	20
Mustard greens, cooked	½ cup	20
Okra, cooked	4 pods, 3 inches long, ⅝ inch in diameter	10
Onions:		
Young, green, raw	6 small, without tops	20
Mature, raw	1 onion, 2½ inches in diameter	40
	1 tablespoon, chopped	5
Mature, cooked	½ cup	30
Parsnips, cooked	½ cup	50

Peas, green:		
Cooked or canned	½ cup	60
Peppers, green:		
Raw or cooked	1 medium	10
Potatoes:		
Baked	1 medium, 2½ inches in diameter (5 ounces raw)	90
Boiled	½ cup, diced	50
Chips (including fat for frying)	10 medium, 2 inches in diameter	115
French-fried (including fat for frying):		
Ready-to-eat	10 pieces, 2 inches by ½ inch by ½ inch	155
Frozen, heated, ready-to-serve	10 pieces, 2 inches by ½ inch by ½ inch	125
Hash-browned	½ cup	225
Mashed:		
Milk added	½ cup	60
Milk and fat added	½ cup	90
Pan-fried, beginning with raw potatoes	½ cup	230
Sweet potatoes:		
Baked in jacket	1 medium, 5 by 2 inches (6 ounces raw)	155
Canned, vacuum or solid pack	½ cup	120
Radishes, raw	4 small	5
Sauerkraut, canned	½ cup	20
Spinach, cooked or canned	½ cup	20
Squash:		
Summer, cooked	½ cup	15
Winter, baked, mashed	½ cup	65
Tomatoes:		
Raw	1 medium, 2 by 2½ inches (about ⅓ pound)	35
Cooked or canned	½ cup	25

Tomato juice, canned	½ cup	20
Turnips, cooked	½ cup	20
Turnip greens, cooked	½ cup	15
Fruits:		
Apples, raw	1 medium, 2½ inches in diameter (about ⅓ pound)	70
Apple juice, canned	½ cup	60
Applesauce:		
Sweetened	½ cup	115
Unsweetened	½ cup	50
Apricots:		
Raw	3 (about 12 to a pound, as purchased)	55
Canned:		
Water pack	½ cup, halves and liquid	45
Heavy syrup pack	½ cup, halves and syrup	110
Dried, cooked, unsweetened	½ cup, fruit and juice	120
Frozen, sweetened	½ cup	125
Avocados:		
California varieties	½ of a 10-ounce avocado (3⅓ by 4¼ inches)	185
Florida varieties	½ of a 13-ounce avocado (4 by 3 inches)	160
Bananas, raw	1 banana (6 by 1½ inches, about ⅓ pound)	85
Berries:		
Blackberries, raw	½ cup	40
Blueberries, raw	½ cup	40
Raspberries:		
Fresh, red, raw	½ cup	35
Frozen, red, sweetened	½ cup	120
Fresh, black, raw	½ cup	50
Strawberries:		
Fresh, raw	½ cup	30

Strawberries:		
Frozen, sweetened	½ cup, sliced	140
Cantaloupe, raw	½ melon,	60
	inches in diameter	
Cherries:		
Raw:		
Sour	½ cup	30
Sweet	½ cup	40
Cranberry sauce, canned, sweetened	1 tablespoon	25
Cranberry juice cocktail, canned	½ cup	80
Dates, "fresh" and dried, pitted, cut	½ cup	245
Figs:		
Raw	3 small (1½ inches in diameter, about ¼ pound)	90
Canned, heavy syrup	½ cup	110
Dried	1 large (2 inches by 1 inch)	60
Fruit cocktail, canned in heavy syrup	½ cup	100
Grapefruit:		
Raw:		
White	½ medium (4¼ inches in diameter)	55
	½ cup sections	40
Pink or red	½ medium (4¼ inches in diameter)	60
Canned:		
Water pack	½ cup	35
Syrup pack	½ cup	90
Grapefruit juice:		
Fresh-squeezed	½ cup	50
Canned:		
Unsweetened	½ cup	50
Sweetened	½ cup	65

Grapefruit juice:		
Frozen concentrate, diluted, ready-to-serve:		
Unsweetened	½ cup	50
Sweetened	½ cup	60
Grapes, raw:		
American type (including Concord, Delaware, Niagara, and Scuppernong), slip skin	1 bunch (3½ by 3 inches; about 3½ ounces)	45
	½ cup, with skins and seeds	30
European type (including Malaga, Muscat, Thompson seedless, and Flame Tokay), adherent skin	½ cup	50
Grapejuice, bottled	½ cup	80
Honeydew melon, raw	1 wedge, 2 by 7 inches	50
Lemon juice, raw or canned	½ cup	30
	1 tablespoon	5
Lemonade, frozen concentrate, sweetened, diluted, ready-to-serve	½ cup	55
Oranges, raw	1 orange, 3 inches in diameter	75
Orange juice:		
Fresh-squeezed	½ cup	55
Canned, unsweetened	½ cup	60
Frozen, concentrate, diluted, ready-to-serve	½ cup	55
Peaches:		
Raw	1 medium, 2 inches in diameter (about ¼ pound)	35
	½ cup, sliced	30

Peaches:		
Canned:		
Water pack	½ cup	40
Heavy syrup pack	½ cup	100
Dried, cooked, unsweetened	½ cup (5 to 6 halves and 3 tablespoons syrup)	110
Frozen, sweetened	½ cup	105
Pears:		
Raw	1 pear, 3 by 2½ inches in diameter	100
Canned in heavy syrup	½ cup	100
Pineapple:		
Raw	½ cup, diced	40
Canned in heavy syrup:		
Crushed	½ cup	100
Sliced	2 small or 1 large slice and 2 tablespoons juice	90
Pineapple juice, canned	½ cup	70
Plums:		
Raw	1 plum, 2 inches in diameter (about 2 ounces)	25
Canned, syrup pack	½ cup	100
Prunes, dried, cooked:		
Unsweetened	½ cup (8 to 9 prunes and 2 tablespoons liquid)	150
Sweetened	½ cup (8 to 9 prunes and 2 tablespoons liquid)	255
Prune juice, canned	½ cup	100
Raisins, dried	½ cup	230
Rhubarb, cooked, sweetened	½ cup	190
Tangerine, raw	1 medium, 2½ inches in diameter (about ¼ pound)	40

Tangerine juice, canned	½ cup	50
Watermelon, raw	1 wedge, 4 by 8 inches long (about 2 pounds, including rind)	115

BREADS AND CEREALS

Bread:		*cals.*
Cracked wheat	1 slice, ½ inch thick	60
Raisin	1 slice, ½ inch thick	60
Rye	1 slice, ½ inch thick	55
White	1 slice, ½ inch thick	60
Whole wheat	1 slice, ½ inch thick	55
Other baked goods:		
Baking powder biscuit	1 biscuit, 2½ inches in diameter	140
Bagels	1	180
Crackers:		
Graham	4 small or 2 medium	55
Saltines	2 crackers, 2 inches square	35
Soda	2 crackers, 2½ inches square	50
Oyster	10 crackers	45
Doughnuts (cake type)	1 doughnut	125
Muffins:		
Plain	1 muffin, 2¾ inches in diameter	140
Bran	1 muffin, 2¾ inches in diameter	130
Corn	1 muffin, 2¾ inches in diameter	150
Pancakes (griddle cakes):		
Wheat (home recipe)	1 cake, 4 inches in diameter	60
Buckwheat (with buckwheat pancake mix)	1 cake, 4 inches in diameter	55

Pizza (cheese)	5½-inch sector, ⅛ of a 14-inch pie	185
Pretzels	5 small sticks	20
Rolls:		
Plain, pan	1 roll (16 ounces per dozen)	115
Hard, round	1 roll (22 ounces per dozen)	160
Sweet, pan	1 roll (18 ounces per dozen)	135
Rye wafers	2 wafers, 1⅞ by 3½ inches	45
Waffles	1 waffle, 4½ by 5½ inches by ½ inch	210
Cereals and other grain products:		
Bran flakes (40-percent bran)	1 ounce (about ⅘ cup)	85
Corn, puffed, pre-sweetened	1 ounce (about 1 cup)	110
Corn, shredded	1 ounce (about ⅘ cup)	110
Corn flakes	1 ounce (about 1⅓ cups)	110
Corn grits, degermed, cooked	¾ cup	90
Farina, cooked	¾ cup	75
Macaroni, cooked	¾ cup	115
Macaroni and cheese	½ cup	235
Noodles, cooked	¾ cup	150
Oat cereal (mixture mainly oat flour)	1 ounce (about 1⅛ cups)	115
Oatmeal, cooked	¾ cup	100
Rice, cooked	¾ cup	140
Rice flakes	1 cup (about 1 ounce)	115
Rice, puffed	1 cup (about ½ ounce)	55
Spaghetti, cooked	¾ cup	115
Spaghetti with meat-balls	¾ cup	250

Spaghetti in tomato sauce, with cheese	¾ cup	195
Wheat, puffed	1 ounce (about 2⅛ cups)	105
Wheat, puffed, presweetened	1 ounce (about 2⅛ cups)	105
Wheat, rolled, cooked	¾ cup	130
Wheat, shredded, plain (long, round, or bite-size)	1 ounce (1 large biscuit or about ½ cup bite-size)	100
Wheat flakes	1 ounce (about ¾ cup)	100
Wheat flours:		
Whole wheat	¾ inch, stirred	300
All-purpose (or family) flour	¾ cup, sifted	300
Wheat germ	¾ cup, stirred	185

FATS, OILS, AND RELATED PRODUCTS

		cals.
Butter or margarine	1 tablespoon	100
	1 pat or square (64 per pound)	50
Cooking fats:		
Vegetable	1 tablespoon	110
Lard	1 tablespoon	125
Salad or cooking oils	1 tablespoon	125
Salad dressings:		
French	1 tablespoon	60
Blue cheese, French	1 tablespoon	80
Home-cooked, boiled	1 tablespoon	30
Low-calorie	1 tablespoon	15
Mayonnaise	1 tablespoon	110
Salad dressing, commercial, plain (mayonnaise-type)	1 tablespoon	65
Thousand Island	1 tablespoon	75

SUGARS, SWEETS, AND RELATED PRODUCTS

		cals.
Candy:		
Caramels	1 ounce (3 medium caramels)	115
Chocolate creams	1 ounce (2 to 3 pieces, 35 to a pound)	125
Chocolate, milk, sweet-ened	1-ounce bar	150
Chocolate, milk, sweet-ened, with almonds	1-ounce bar	150
Chocolate mints	1 ounce (1 to 2 mints, 20 to a pound)	115
Fudge, milk chocolate, plain	1 ounce (1 piece, 1 to 1½ inches square)	115
Gumdrops	1 ounce (about 2½ large or 20 small)	100
Hard candy	1 ounce (3 to 4 candy balls, ¾ inch in diameter)	110
Jellybeans	1 ounce (10 beans)	105
Marshmallows	1 ounce (3 to 4 marsh-mallows, 60 to a pound)	90
Peanut brittle	1 ounce (1½ pieces, 2½ by 1¼ inches by ⅜ inch)	120
Syrup, honey, molasses:		
Chocolate syrup	1 tablespoon	50
Honey, strained or extracted	1 tablespoon	65
Molasses, cane, light	1 tablespoon	50
Syrup, table blends	1 tablespoon	60
Jelly	1 tablespoon	55
Jam, marmalade, preserves	1 tablespoon	55
Sugar: white, granu-lated, or brown	1 teaspoon	15

SOUPS		*cals.*
Bean with pork	1 cup	170
Beef noodle	1 cup	70
Bouillon, broth, and consomme	1 cup	30
Chicken noodle	1 cup	65
Clam chowder	1 cup	85
Cream of mushroom	1 cup	135
Minestrone	1 cup	105
Oyster stew	1 cup (3 to 4 oysters)	200
Tomato	1 cup	90
Vegetable with beef broth	1 cup	80

DESSERTS		*cals.*
Apple betty	½ cup	170
Cakes:		
Angel food cake	2-inch sector (1/12 of 8-inch round cake)	110
Butter cakes:		
Plain, without icing	1 piece, 3 by 2 by 1½ inches	200
	1 cupcake, 2¾ inches in diameter	145
Plain, with chocolate icing	2-inch sector (1/16 of 10-inch round layer cake)	370
	1 cupcake, 2¾ inches in diameter	185
Chocolate, with chocolate icing	2-inch sector (1/16 of 10-inch round layer cake)	445
Fruitcake, dark	1 piece, 2 by 2 inches by ½ inch	115
Gingerbread	1 piece, 2 by 2 by 2 inches	175
Pound cake	1 slice, 2¾ by 3 inches by 5/8 inch	140
Sponge cake	2-inch sector (1/12 of 8-inch round cake)	120

Cookies, plain and assorted	1 cookie, 3 inches in diameter	120
Cornstarch pudding	½ cup	140
Custard, baked	½ cup	140
Figbars, small	1 figbar	55
Fruit ice	½ cup	75
Gelatin dessert, plain, ready-to-serve	½ cup	70
Ice cream, plain	1 container (3½ fluid ounces)	130
Ice milk	½ cup (4 fluid ounces)	140
Pies:		
Apple	4-inch sector (⅐ of 9-inch pie)	345
Cherry	4-inch sector (⅐ of 9-inch pie)	355
Custard	4-inch sector (⅐ of 9-inch pie)	280
Lemon meringue	4-inch sector (⅐ of 9-inch pie)	305
Mince	4-inch sector (⅐ of 9-inch pie)	365
Pumpkin	4-inch sector (⅐ of 9-inch pie)	275
Prune whip	½ cup	105
Rennet dessert pudding, ready-to-serve	½ cup	130
Sherbet	½ cup	130

Notes

1. W. H. Dietz and S. L. Gortmaker. "Do we fatten our children at the television set? Obesity and television viewing in children and adolescents." *Pediatrics*, 1985, *75*, 807–812.

2. S. Dalvit-McPhillips. "A dietary approach to bulimia treatment." *Physiology & Behavior*, 1984, *33*, 769–775.

3. A. R. Weiss. "A behavioral approach to the treatment of adolescent obesity." *Behavior Therapy*, 1977, *8*, 720–726.

4. R. S. Paffenbarger, R. T. Hyde, A. L. Wing, and C. Hsieh, "Physical activity, all-cause mortality, and longevity of college alumni." *New England Journal of Medicine*, 1986, *314*, 605–613.

Suggested
Readings

Bailey, Covert. *Fit or Fat?* Boston: Houghton Mifflin, 1978.

(This is a short and readable book that provides, in simple terms, scientific explanations about how diet and exercise affect the body. It has a very good discussion on how to develop a safe exercise program.)

Edelstein, Barbara. *The Woman Doctor's Diet for Teenage Girls.* Englewood Cliffs, New Jersey: Prentice-Hall, 1980.

(This is an excellent treatment of the special problems faced by teenage girls today. It covers the pressure to be thin, healthy alternatives to fad diets, and how girls can handle the food situations they commonly encounter without putting on excess weight.)

Gardner, Joseph L., *Eat Better, Live Better: A Commonsense Guide to Nutrition and Good Health.* Pleasantville, New York: Reader's Digest Association, 1982.

(This is a large book, but it is written in *Reader's Digest* simplified style. It contains a large number of pictures of food, recipes, tables of how much of each nutrient can be found in various foods, and so on. This book is a good place to start for general nutrition knowledge.)

Kolodny, Nancy J. *When Food's a Foe: Eating Disorders Explained and Exposed.* Boston: Little, Brown, 1987.

(This book provides an explanation of eating disorders from a teenager's point of view. It includes the causes and effects of eating disorders as well as how they can be overcome.)

Stuart, Richard B., and Barbara Davis. *Slim Chance in a Fat World: Behavioral Control of Obesity.* Champaign, Illinois: Research Press, 1978.

(The condensed edition of this book is short and readable. It emphasizes behavioral control of eating habits, providing numerous valuable suggestions to help you break bad habits and build better ones.)

Woolfolk, Dorothy A. *The Teenage Surefire Diet Cookbook.* New York: Franklin Watts, 1979.

(This book provides scores of simple diet recipes for meat, fish, poultry, and egg dishes as well as soups, salads, salad dressings, etc.)

Index